Blueprint for Screenwriting

A Complete Writer's Guide to Story Structure and Character Development

Typo: 126, 127, 129

Blueprint for Screenwriting

A Complete Writer's Guide to Story Structure and Character Development

Rachel Ballon, PhD

LAWRENCE ERLBAUM ASSOCIATES, PUBLISHERS
2005   Mahwah, New Jersey   London

Lawrence Erlbaum Associates, Inc., Publishers
10 Industrial Avenue
Mahwah, New Jersey 07430

Cover design by Kathryn Houghtaling Lacey

Library of Congress Cataloging-in-Publication Data

Ballon, Rachel Friedman. Blueprint for screenwriting : a writer's guide to creativity, craft, and career / Rachel Ballon.—2nd ed.
      p. cm.
Rev. ed. of: Blueprint for writing. c1994.
      Includes bibliographical references and index.
ISBN 0-8058-4922-X (cloth : alk. paper)
ISBN 0-8058-4923-8 (pbk. : alk. paper)
1. Motion picture authorship.   I. Ballon, Rachel Friedman. Blueprint for writing.   II. Title.
PN1996.B37   2004
808.2'3—dc22   2004046929
                                                                CIP

Books published by Lawrence Erlbaum Associates are printed on acid-free paper, and their bindings are chosen for strength and durability.

Printed in the United States of America
10   9   8   7   6   5   4   3   2

Contents

Preface: Blueprint for Screenwriting **vii**

Chapter 1 Creativity: Your Blueprint for Ideas **1**

Chapter 2 Building Your Story **11**

Chapter 3 Constructing Your Blueprint: Laying Down the Framework **20**

Chapter 4 Story Structure: The Screenplay's Foundation **31**

Chapter 5 The Main Character **39**

Chapter 6 Characters and Conflict **49**

Chapter 7 Creating the Character's Emotional Arc: The Heart of the Story **58**

Chapter 8 The Psychology of Characters **67**

Chapter 9   Structuring Scenes and Acts   **77**

Chapter 10   The Outline, the Treatment, The Synopsis   **88**

Chapter 11   Script Format   **96**

Chapter 12   Dialogue   **106**

Chapter 13   Subtext   **114**

Chapter 14   Writing From Your Inner Cast   **124**
                 of Characters

Chapter 15   Overcoming Writer's Block   **136**

Chapter 16   The Completed Screenplay   **150**

                 Afterword: How to Survive   **153**
                   the Writing Game

                 Index   **167**

Preface: Blueprint for Screenwriting

"The inner shape of a man's life is what he writes from and about."
—Ross MacDonald

Blueprint for Screenwriting is designed for anyone who wants to write a screenplay from beginning screenplay writers to professionals writers. It is for you writers who want to have a blueprint to refer to when you write your script, so you'll have the correct story structure and extensive knowledge of character development.

If you complete the *Blueprint for Screenwriting* exercises given to you at the end of each chapter you will master the craft of structuring a story for films and television movies. Your blueprint will enable you to take your original idea and work it through until you have a completed screenplay, which will be professionally written and structured. Your well-crafted screenplay will showcase your writing ability and illustrate that you know how to structure your writing and develop memorable characters.

Think of yourself as the architect of your screenplay. Just as an architect first creates a blueprint before constructing a building, you, too, must create a blueprint before constructing your script. A blueprint keeps you headed in the right direction, gives structure to your story and allows you to master the step-by-step techniques necessary for writing a successful script.

Most people have the mistaken notion that writing a screenplay is easy, until they try to write one. They soon discover they don't know what to do next and usually give up after realizing how difficult it really is. How many of you have tried to write a feature film or television movie and failed? Did you get bogged down in the middle, have trouble developing the right structure, or just didn't know what to do? You probably got frustrated and quit, because you didn't know where to go, how to get there and what to do next. These problems happened because you didn't have a plan or a blueprint to follow.

This book will act as your guide and show you how to develop the right story structure before you start writing your screenplay. By building your blueprint first, every time you start a screenplay it will not be written by accident or chance, but through the knowledge of craft you'll learn in this book.

I first began teaching screenplay writing workshops at UCLA extension in the Writer's Program over twenty years ago and also conducted screenwriting seminars at the American Film Institute in Los Angeles. Eventually, I became an adjunct Professor in the highly-respected School of Cinema and Television at University of Southern California, where I taught screenwriting and character development to writing students in the film school.

Over the past two decades I've taught thousands of screenplay writers throughout the United States and Europe how to create a blueprint for screenwriting. These writing workshops were always well attended and it was not surprising that so many people wanted to learn the craft of screenwriting. The film and television industries afford writers great financial opportunities that few other industries offer. Where else can an unknown writer break in at the top by selling a million dollar script?

All it takes to make you an overnight success is just one exciting, fabulous script. Sounds easy enough doesn't it? Well, it isn't! Like all overnight successes you must first pay your dues by learning plot, dialogue, theme, narrative, exposition, visual imagery, sound, action, and mastering the craft of story, with an emphasis on structure and character development.

Of course, if you don't want to sell your script that's just fine—to just write for your self. However, most writers who consulted with me about their screenplay did so because they wanted to write the best one possible, so that a producer or studio executive would turn it into a motion picture. It wasn't just for the money, but because they wanted to share their vision and point-of-view with audiences throughout the world. So you see, it isn't mutually exclusive to want to be commercial and to also want to write a great script. In fact, if you don't write a terrific screenplay you won't sell it. In either case you still want to write a great script.

Originally, I wrote this book for the thousands of writing students taking my workshops and classes who wanted to refer to my lectures. I self-published my classroom exercises in a book called *Blueprint For Writing* to be used by writers as a helpful resource for them to create a blueprint to follow when writing. In fact, I used it as the text for my screenplay writing classes at USC Film School and other universities.

My purpose for writing *Blueprint For Screenwriting* is to teach you how to "demystify" the writing process. I want to give writers who haven't taken my workshops the same tools I have given my students: to develop a blueprint to follow every time you start a new screenplay—from original concept through to completed script.

Many individuals who attend my workshops were people already working in the industry. Some are screenplay writers, producers, assistant directors, readers, development executives, actors, and editors. Why do all these people take writing courses in structure and character development if they are already in the business? Surprisingly enough, many of them don't know how to structure a script and want to learn the basics of what it takes to create a great story and develop realistic and memorable characters.

After following the principles in *Blueprint for Screenwriting* many students have had their screenplays optioned or sold. Some have gotten staff positions on situation comedies and hour episodic dramas for television. Others have received writing assignments from production companies and networks, after their screenplays were read by story editors and producers. They received assignments because the development executives or producers recognized these writers understood the basics of screenplay writing. These entertainment industry executives were willing to risk money on these writers, because they had proven themselves to be capable of laying out a plot structure and develop credible characters.

If you want to be a successful writer it doesn't matter whether or not you have prior writing experience. What does matter is a willingness to learn the fundamentals of screenwriting and to work hard developing your craft. Those who succeed as screenwriters never give up but write and rewrite and rewrite. They have the most important ingredient for writing success—perseverance and a strong desire to become a screenwriter. They are able to call themselves writers because they have mastered their craft by doing the difficult work of writing and not because they just want to be known as writers!

This book is written for those of you who don't happen to live in Hollywood, California, or New York City, New York, where many classes in screenplay writing are taught. It is for you who live in Bellefonte, Pennsylvania, or Duluth, Minnesota, or Palm Beach, Florida and want to learn an easy-to-follow method of writing. A method that will work over and over again.

By working *Blueprint for Screenwriting*, you will have a step-by-step plan and guide to follow every inch of the way—from getting started to completing your script. This book can be a creative tool for you. All you need to do is work it! By doing so you'll develop your ability as a writer. Your finished screenplay will be the calling card you need to open doors for you! You'll be able to call yourself a screenwriter, because you will know how to build your story, develop credible characters and put them into a solid structure which works over and over again.

Chapter 1

Creativity: Your Blueprint for Ideas

"Ideas we don't know we have, have us."

—James Hill

Story structure and character development are the architecture for building your blueprint. Without a solid structure your characters will be transparent. And without multidimensional characters your structure will collapse. You may ask as thousands of writers do: "Which comes first the structure or the character?" My response to that question is, "Neither."

To me character is structure and structure is character. How can you possibly separate the two? This is like saying which came first, the chicken or the egg? It is through a character's choices, decisions and actions that a plot or structure is created. Plot is character and character is plot. They are synergistic and just go together.

However, before learning about plot and character, you need to have ideas about what you want to write. And believe it or not many writers aren't able to access any ideas for their screenplay. Why? They aren't able to reach their own creativity or imagination, because they're not allowing the creativity to flow since they're too analytical too soon in the writing process.

On the other hand, I've worked with writers who had many ideas they wanted to write and yet had trouble developing a story for their ideas. In other cases, writers had the story they wanted to write, but had no idea how to develop the characters needed for their story.

CREATIVITY AND IMAGINATION

So how do you get ideas for your screenplay? Where do ideas for your screenplay come from? Well, it has to do with your own imagination and from your creativity. What is creativity? Creativity is free-flowing energy and when you are connected to your own inner world, where your creativity resides, you will find a myriad of ideas for your screenplays.

Creativity has to be available to you at the beginning of your writing because without creative ideas, concepts, or thoughts you have nothing to write about and can't start any writing project.

Creativity is where all poetry, art, drama, music and ideas come from that touch people on a deep emotional level. Creativity is made up of two parts. First there is Primary Creativity which comes from your unconscious and the right hemisphere of your brain, the source of all new ideas and insights. It's where your inspiration comes from and makes up only 10% of the creative process. Then, there is Secondary Creativity, which comes from the left hemisphere and is the 90% that involves editing, discipline, logic, structure, rewriting, and order.

Creativity includes both inspiration and perspiration and as a writer you need to discover how to combine the elements of art or primary creativity, with the elements of craft or secondary creativity. Both components are necessary to be a fully creative writer and you need to strike a balance between the two. For example, if an automobile is to run smoothly you must have all the parts working together. If the engine breaks down, a tire goes flat or you run out of gas, your car won't run. Each part depends upon the other.

The same is true for writing. If you can access your creativity and come up with more ideas than you know what to do with, but you don't know how to put them into a craft or a structure, your writing will break down, too. If you know craft, but have blocked your creativity your writing will be flat and your characters will be weak and run out of gas. And finally, you must have respect for structure which is necessary to transform your shapeless inner world into a concrete blueprint or your writing will stall.

To be a productive and successful screenwriter you must write from both your heart and from your head, the basis of all great writing. Writing from your heart enables you to increase your creative output and allows you to reveal who you truly are and put it in your writing. When you write from your heart the writing is passionate, original, and honest. It has greater intensity and depth of emotions, which enables your audience to identify with your screenplay.

To be a more creative writer is to have the courage to return to your childhood memories, where you were freer and less self-conscious, than you probably are now. When you first begin to write allow that spontaneous creative side of you to emerge through your words without criticizing or analyzing your writing.

Abraham H. Maslow, author of *The Farther Reaches of the Human Nature* said in an October, 1962 lecture:

> The creative attitude requires both courage and strength and most studies of creative people have reported one or another version of courage … that becoming more courageous makes it easier to let oneself be attracted by mystery, by the unfamiliar … by the ambiguous and contradictory, by the universal and unexpected.

In childhood the fusion of primary and secondary creativity is found in us, but unfortunately lost in most of us as we grow up and as adults learn to hide our true self behind the many masks we wear. To become more creative is to allow yourself the opportunity to become a playful, joyous child, to be courageous and not afraid, to let go and have fun with your writing. By allowing your child to come out and play when you first begin to write, you'll be less judgmental, constricted, and rigid about your writing, and hopefully the words will flow.

Writing From Your Heart

I have worked with all level of writers, from rank beginners to experienced professionals, who were too into the results of their writing, before they even had written their script. This attitude stopped them in their creative process before they ever got started.

You need to be in the moment when you write and not into the results. When you first begin to develop your blueprint for screen-writing, you mustn't block yourself with criticisms and judgments before you get your ideas down on the page. If you do, you will stop yourself too soon in the writing process and not finish writing your script. It's important to suspend your judgment until after you've written down your ideas, your story, or your concept. Otherwise, you will not be able to start writing your screenplay let alone complete it.

When you begin to develop your screenplay, concentrate on the writing process itself and not on the technique. Write down your ideas without worrying whether or not they're good enough. By writing in the moment you'll lose your past and future and your ideas will flow. This way of writing from your heart is the first burst of creative imagination that comes to you in a moment of insight or a burst of inspiration.

Have you ever started to write and when you looked at the clock hours had gone by when you thought you'd only been working for minutes? That's because you were being in the moment, totally immersed and absorbed in the present. You were involved in the process of writing, rather than worrying about the product or results.

To be a productive and successful writer you must write from both your heart and your head, the basis of all great writing. This type of writing enables you to increase your creative output and allows you to reveal who you truly are and put it into your writing. To be a fully creative writer you must be open to all aspects of yourself, since repression of your feelings works against your creativity. If you avoid looking inside yourself, you'll lose parts of yourself and your past experiences and you won't be able or willing to put those fertile ideas and feelings into your writing. This will prevent you from reconnecting to your inner self.

Journals to Reconnect with Your Inner Self.

An excellent way for reconnecting with your inner self is to write in a journal. I tell both writing students and therapy clients to start writing in a journal. It doesn't have to be one of those fancy notebooks or one of those expensive handmade books. Just buy a simple notebook, preferably one you can carry around with you at all times. A journal is a wonderful tool for helping you monitor yourself— what you're thinking, feeling, and dreaming about throughout the day and night. Get into the habit of writing in your journal every day. Record your thoughts, feelings, ideas, and even your dreams (both the day and the night ones).

Some writers who've consulted with me have kept many different journals for specific reasons. One woman had a dream journal, a daily journal, and a journal for childhood stories. Another writer had an idea journal recording dialogue, concepts, and plots from his daily life for use in his scripts.

CAUTION!

I wholly recommend journals for non-writers, too. They are a wonderful bridge between your external and internal selves. The only caution is not to write in your journal just when you're feeling depressed. Many people use a journal to dump their feelings and it gets to be a bad habit. To counteract this habit I suggest that you buy a journal and call it your "Joyful Journal," and write about only those situations that make you feel good.

Another type of journal you might want to create is a writer's journal. In this type of journal you can make different headings and sections according to dialogue, plot, ideas, characters, settings, and atmosphere. Keep this journal with you and you'll be surprised how much more observant you'll become of people, places, and events throughout your day. Writers need to be keen observers of human behavior. What better way to heighten your ability to record human nature than to write in your journal. You'll be pleasantly surprised how many ideas you'll get for your future screenplays just from being aware of your surroundings and the people in them. You'll see how much material you'll discover at work, from friends, family, and in your personal relationships.

KEEP A DREAM JOURNAL FOR STORY IDEAS

A young man who was working on his masters degree in film school asked me to consult with him on his final project before graduation—a short film. He couldn't think of anything to write until we had a session in which he told me about a couple of his dreams. I suggested that he begin to record his dreams in a dream journal and then read them to me. From writing down his dreams as soon as he awakened, so not to forget them, he discovered a dream which he could use as the basis for his short film. He wrote his short film from his dream and when he completed it, his film won several awards at film festivals. He would never have achieved writing about something that came from the inside out and was meaningful to him without first creating his dream journal and making the commitment to use it as a writing resource. His short film stood out from the rest because it was personal and passionate to the writer and therefore to the audience.

CHILDHOOD
JOURNAL Another client, an experienced professional had already sold several screenplays. She came to see me because she felt her writing was shallow and wanted to write with more emotional intensity. We began working on her childhood experiences which she recorded in her personal journal. One day she brought in a particular traumatic event and we discussed how it related to her childhood. She took the germ of her painful childhood experience and wrote a screenplay from it. The script emerged from her passion, her childhood, her truth and her emotions. She wrote about something that came from the inside out and was meaningful to her. Her screenplay was made into an award winning film which stands out from other films, because it's personal, passionate and honest.

I have consulted with many experienced professionals who have already had success yet when starting a new script become blocked and unable to write, because they're afraid to connect to their inner world. Although they know craft they avoid tapping their inner feelings and resist getting in touch with their emotions. Their writing remains stilted, their characters clichéd and they'll have problems selling their script, until they're willing to express themselves and reveal who they are through their characters.

Visualization and Free Writing

To enable you to reach your inner depths, and a well-spring of new ideas, I will lead you in a writing exercise. You will begin the journey to travel beneath your mask and mine your childhood stories, memories, intention, and emotions, through using visualization and free writing.

Visualization is the technique of imagining visual pictures. It closes off the left hemisphere of your brain and lets the right hemisphere express insights and inspirations without criticisms. Visualization also involves the exploration of pictures that come to your mind allowing you to experience a kind of waking dream.

Before you begin your visualization, first get comfortable, close your eyes and begin to relax by breathing deeply. If you wish you may listen to relaxing music, such as Yoga or mediation tapes. Continue breathing until you feel the muscles in your body relax completely. After you are totally relaxed, visualize yourself as a small child. Picture yourself in a natural setting such as in a meadow, a park, the woods, or by the ocean. As you visualize, become part of the scene with all of your senses. Smell the sea air, listen to the birds singing, hear the wind rustling through the leaves, see the myriad colors of the ocean and taste the salty water. Really get into the scene and imagine yourself being there with all of your senses. What are you wearing? How does you hair look? What expression do you have on your face? Are you alone or with a friend? Take a few more moments and visualize what you're feeling in this wonderful childhood place. Are you happy? Sad? Lonely? Playful? Free?

Now take your pen and start writing about the experience. Using first person (I), present tense (am), write with all your senses, describing the visual pictures you experienced. Do not stop writing until you've written for twenty minutes. Do not take your pen from the page and don't read over anything you've written until you're finished. It's important for you to be free when you write and not to worry about grammar, spelling or punctuation.

If you get stuck and can't think of anything else to write, then write about feeling stuck and not being able to write. No matter what—don't stop writing until at least twenty minutes have passed. If you want, you could set a timer and not stop until it goes off. Writing about this waking dream *without* any type of structure or rules, enables you to access powerfully dramatic stories and memories from your past.

This type of writing, which is known as free or automatic writing, when combined with visualization offers a direct path to the unconscious and to your buried treasures—emotions, feelings, memories.

WRITING FROM THE HEART, WRITING FROM THE HEAD

In my *Writing From the Heart, Writing From the Head* workshops, I spend the first day showing writers how to tap into their inner world by doing these specific writing exercises. By going on this visual journey many writers come up with extraordinary images they record through the written word, describing all the details through their sense of smell, sight, sound, taste and touch. Afterwards, they take their childhood memories and stories and transform them into fictional characters and plots.

Many writers were surprised at both the quality and power of this type of free writing. Others never approached writing from this perspective of dealing first with creativity and found this technique allowed them to write with greater ease and intensity. Stories that they needed to write became accessible to them through free writing.

My main objective for having you write this way is to get you to write *your* truth, to write *your* passion, by taking your memories and transforming them into well-structured, stories that emotionally move others. After you've completed writing about your childhood memory, see if you can put it into a story or a scene. When you write from this powerful source you will be able to create fresh stories and original characters who come alive.

A tool for self-knowledge and self-discovery, free writing allows you to self-explore your unconscious. Not only will your writing improve, but through writing your childhood stories you will be on the path of healing unfinished business. By dealing with your past through writing, will make you feel better and also relieve stress.

Remember, when you begin to write you just want to get your creative ideas down on the page without the self-consciousness of your judgmental self. When you analyze and criticize your writing too soon in the writing process you may become blocked. So silence your critic by continuing to write without editing your work, no matter what! This free writing must be done without self-criticism. There is certainly plenty of time for that to come when you're re-writing. In the beginning just write without censoring your thoughts, feelings, or ideas before you ask yourself the following:

"Is it good?" "Does it work?" "Will it sell?"

The only thing you should be concerned with at the beginning of your writing journey is to get your words down on the page. Just get out of the way of your creative self and trust the process. Successful writers have an openness to themselves and their writing. Trust the process without being self-conscious and you will end up rich with imagination, spontaneity, and creativity, all the ingredients you need for screenwriting success.

When you are able to write from the inside out, your writing is more honest and has greater feeling, because you aren't forcing it or trying to be brilliant. I always tell writers when they first begin a screenplay: "It doesn't have to be right, just WRITE it!"   SLOGAN

Your creativity must be nurtured. It is one of the real gifts in life that is also free for the taking. It's up to you to untie the bow and open your gift each and every day! Before you know it you'll have more story ideas then you ever thought possible.

BLUEPRINT FOR SCREENWRITING

10 TIPS TO IMPROVE YOUR CREATIVITY

1. Start the day with a new approach. Instead of writing on your computer try a legal pad with pen, because you will write more naturally without worrying about a mechanical process. Get a change of scenery and don't write at your desk, just go out in nature and relax.
2. Put on relaxing music when you write and put the rhythms of the music into the rhythms of your words.
3. Trust your "gut feelings" and your natural instincts when you first start to write. Learn to rely more on your intuition than your logic.
4. Take a break from your writing and go for a walk on your favorite path. Take time to discover new things you've never seen before—pretend you're a tourist this time.
5. Take five to fifteen minutes a day to daydream. Really allow your imagination to soar and let your playful child come out then write from your child's voice.
6. Read poetry for at least 10 minutes before you begin to write. Nursery rhymes are especially good, because they have a natural rhythm and meter, which connects you to your creativity.
7. Visit the ocean, a river or park and write a brief paragraph about your experience. Describe the colors, sounds, and smells of nature in words using your sense of touch, taste, sound, sight and smell.
8. Set a timer for at least twenty minutes when you first start to write. Don't stop writing until the timer goes off. This automatic writing will help you avoid being critical or judgmental.
9. Start a journal and write in it daily. Record your feelings and thoughts as well as noting your behavior and relationships. This will sharpen your observation skills.
10. Start a dream journal and record your day dreams as well as your night dreams. Your dreams will provide you with a wealth of material for your writing projects. Listen to your dreams— you created them!

Chapter 2

Building Your Story

"I write entirely to find out what I am thinking, what I want, and what I fear."

—Joan Didion

YOUR MOTIVES FOR WRITING

As a screenwriter you're not only the creator of your screenplay, but your choice of material will either make the experience an exciting adventure or an agonizing voyage. This chapter deals with the most important element in the writing process—YOU, the writer.

It's important to look at your motives for wanting to write, because if they aren't strong enough you probably won't finish your screenplay. Writing is just too difficult a craft to learn if you aren't serious about it. So before you begin your writing journey it's necessary for you to answer the following questions:

- Do you know why you want to write?
- Do you want to make a lot of money?
- Do you want to be famous?
- Do you want to get recognition?
- Do you want to entertain others?

- Do you want only to be known as a writer without writing?

If these are your only reasons for wanting to become a writer give it up now, because they're all the wrong reasons. However, you may feel you have something important to say and want to share it with others. Perhaps you want to tell people about your strong feelings and beliefs through the written word. Or maybe you have a burning desire to tell your personal story. If deep down inside you feel you must write, that you can't live without writing, then writing is for you.

The famous writer Rainer Maria Rilke gave the following advice to an aspiring writer in his book *Letters to a Young Poet*:

> This above all—ask yourself in the stillest hour of your night: 'Must I write?' And if this should be affirmative, if you may meet this earnest question with a strong and simple 'I must,' then build your life according to this necessity: your life even into its most indifferent and slightest hour must be a sign of this urge and a testimony to it.

Do you feel the same way he described? If the answer for you is "I must," then writing a screenplay is what you should do.

In my writing classes I have students answer the question: "WHY I WRITE" The following is an excerpt from this exercise by one of my writing students:

> Writing is a wonderful tool for me to dig out buried feelings that I always try to hide from everyone. But on the page I can let them flow. I can release my pent-up pain, my passion, my hurts, my joys and my fears. When I see what I've written in black and white, the words bear witness to me and validate who I am. Writing awakens my dormant selves and gives voice to them on the page. Writing cuts my spirit free. The words free me from my pain, shame, and blame. What's the point of writing without telling the truth? What's the point of being afraid to expose and to reveal myself on the page? At least when I write I can be free to be the who I want to be, something I don't do in my life. The words are my lifeline for healing myself. I am finally ready to face my fears through my writing and find my true self. I'll write about my story and not another person's story. I am ready to take the journey to meet my true self and my spirit through writing.

As you can see, writing is absolutely meaningful and necessary in this person's life. She is a talented writer who has just finished her second screenplay about discovering her real self through writing. In her screenplay her main character transforms from low self-esteem to feeling confident about herself. It is a wonderful, uplifting coming of age script. It's personal and yet professionally written from the heart.

KEEPING IT PERSONAL

Writing must be personal or it is not worth writing. However, some writers have problems writing the personal story. Many times it is too frightening for them to express their inner emotions such as: love, hate, fear, joy, sorrow, anger or despair. These feelings are very private and at first you may be afraid of exposing your emotions in your script. But to become a successful writer you must be willing to reveal your true self—who you are, what you feel and what you fear.

If you are unable to do this, you have already failed as a writer. No matter how exciting your screenplay may be, if it doesn't have emotional characters no one will care to see it on the screen. Your audience wants to be involved with your characters, to identify with their problems and to root for them.

Take your time before building your story and give a lot of serious consideration to your subject matter. To capture your audience, you must touch them in a deep emotional way, all the more reason for you to be open and honest. Above all, you should write what you know. Don't try to write a story about life being in the Foreign Legion if you have no idea what that entails.

However, if you have a burning desire to write about a subject of which you know nothing and you want to write it no matter what, then do the necessary research before you start writing! Use the library, the Internet and leave no stone unturned until you have full knowledge about your subject. If you don't do extensive research, your story will fall apart, because it won't ring true and nobody will want to buy an admission ticket to see it.

A Balance Between Personal and Professional *writing*

On the other hand, there has to be a balance between being too personal and being so close to your story that you can't be objective.

You can write 90% of your story w/o doing exhaustive preliminary research. Then do target research, interviews, etc to fill the missing jargon, details, info, etc.

What do I mean by this? Well, there are some writers who are so obsessed with writing their personal story that they can't get the objective distance to make their screenplay work.

When I've critiqued writers who write scripts that are too personal, they usually become defensive. "But that's how it really happened," they argue when they receive constructive criticism. Guess what? It really doesn't matter if that's how it really happened, unless one's writing a documentary script.

These writers were just too personally involved in the story to be able to look at it with the necessary objectivity of a professional "writer's eye." It's important to have distance from your subject matter in order to make the necessary changes and revisions to make your screenplay a great one.

However, when the wounds are too raw, writing about the personal experience can be like rubbing "salt in the wound." This is what happened to a middle-age man, whom I'll call Jack. He wanted to write a script about a recently widowed man struggling to be on his own. The main character, married for 26 years, was trying to be independent and deal with all of the problems besetting a man living alone. He had to learn to cook, clean and develop a new social life, while still experiencing the painful feelings of divorce.

Jack had a lot of problems trying to write his story and couldn't get a handle on it. I spoke with him and soon discovered that he was too close to the story, because he was actually going through the pains of his wife's recent death. Every time he'd write a particular scene he'd begin to re-experience his pain all over again. Since he wasn't detached and couldn't get enough distance to look at his screenplay objectively he couldn't write it. In reality, Jack was writing his actual life story as he was living it. This didn't make for an exciting script and his writing wasn't dramatic. It also wasn't healthy for him to write about such a painful situation so soon after it had occurred.

When other students began to give him suggestions he would respond defensively, "Well, that's the way it really happened." He was too emotionally involved with his own real life drama to maintain the necessary distance from his work.

I finally persuaded Jack to put his script aside for the time being and write about something else that wasn't so emotionally upsetting. He eventually chose another story that wasn't so personal, but one which interested him.

With his new story Jack was finally able to become objective and listen to advice from others as he worked on his script. He wasn't defensive and he made changes without getting angry. I began to notice a real change in Jack's personality as he worked on his new script. He soon began to enjoy working on his new screenplay so much, that it helped him forget a lot of his own personal pain. He became less depressed and more optimistic about his own future.

I know some day Jack will probably go back and write his original story about his wife's death. It could make a good script, but not until he is emotionally removed enough to write it and remain dispassionate about the subject.

Jack certainly isn't the only writer I know who eventually had to give up a story. There's really a fine balance between writing what you know and being able to keep the proper emotional distance from your work. Each of you should strive to look at your work as a professional writer and choose material that has meaning for you and which allows you to make changes when you have to without any resistance.

What is also important is for you to take a personal story and make it dramatic and entertaining, while putting your truth into it. You can only do this if you are passionate about your story, yet objective enough to change it if it doesn't work.

DON'T TRY TO BE COMMERCIAL

Before building your story, I want to caution you about what not to write. It is inevitable in every workshop that one student will ask,

"How do I know what the networks or studios are buying?"

"You don't know!" I exclaim.

"What's commercial this year?"

"Nobody knows," I reply.

To want to be commercial or imitate former successful high concept scripts is not a good enough reason to build your story. By the time you write what you think will be a hot topic you'll already be too late. How can you outguess the networks and studios who have staffs on their payroll just to read the newspapers, magazines and manuscripts of books even before they reach the public? You just can't, so don't even try.

Do you recall what happened with the real life Elizabeth Smart kidnapping? Immediately after she was safely found there was a TV movie that was in the works. At the same time another studio made a true-to-life movie about Jessica Lynch who was stationed with the military in Iraq. She was kidnapped in Iraq when the convoy she was in became lost. She was badly injured and alone as a captive of the Iraqis. In a surprise and covert mission she was rescued by a group from the military and she later became known as a hero. Her story was on television the same night as the movie about Elizabeth Smart. Get the picture?

There's really no way to compete with the big conglomerates about current hot topics in the news. These companies even have writers on the payroll who have already started scripts about worldwide hot topics that are seen on the news programs day and night. The writers are just waiting for the actual ending of the real life story, so they are able to complete their screenplay with the correct facts.

Can you recall all the other movies that were released almost immediately after a major newsworthy event or death of a celebrity? And now that we have so many reality talk shows, entertainment exposés on television and all those supermarket tabloids, there is NOTHING you'll be able to get that will scoop these studios or networks, unless of course, you do something sensational and then you'll probably sell your story to the highest bidder.

Hopefully, you can now understand why it doesn't pay to try to be commercial when you write your screenplay. You'll just be wasting your time. You'll never sell the overdone, cliched work you're sure will be commercial, because it's been done over and over again. But you'll always be commercial when you write something new, fresh and original—something that comes from your life experiences, from your heart.

Recently, I conducted a workshop at Screenwriting Expo in Los Angeles. It was called, "The Inside Story: Writing What Hollywood Wants." It was a full house because I'm certain everybody there wanted to learn what was going to sell. However, I'm sure they were surprised when I revealed that what they needed to write was the personal story which nobody else could write. One that would be filled with passion, vision and emotion and be fresh and original—a story that would touch the hearts of the audience.

When you pick your subject matter for your story, it's better to write a contemporary piece and to avoid the epic, or period piece as they are too costly and seldom made, especially by an unknown writer.

There are no new plots under the sun. All have been done over and over again, but not by you. So go for the story that will be uniquely yours. Write one that will be fresh and novel, featuring your point-of-view. Make it a work with originality by writing what you know and revealing who you are. Your personal involvement will make your story come alive and your voice will make a difference and needs to be heard!

By writing about your passion it will be reflected in your screenplay, making it fresh and unique with you. Your screenplay will have a chance of becoming a success, because of your commitment to your story and your need to share your feelings with others.

Assuming that you now have given up the notion of wanting to be commercial just for the sake of being commercial, I want to make it clear that doesn't mean you don't want to sell your screenplay. Of course you probably do or else you wouldn't be writing one. By writing about a story or event that has meaning to you and knowing the correct structure and the elements of dramaturgy, you'll end up with a successful screenplay.

TRANSFORMING PERSONAL STORIES
TO POWERFUL SCRIPTS

✗ Am I entertaining? Am I entertaining?

When you decide on the story you want to write, it is an absolute necessity to put yourself in the position of your audience, asking yourself, "Will they understand what I'm writing?" "Am I getting my point across?" "Am I being objective?" "Am I too emotionally involved?"

If you're only writing for yourself, forget about writing to sell and write in a journal or a diary. No one is interested in your latest love affair or break up. Write about them in your journal! Your first goal as a professional writer is to entertain your audience. A professional writer takes the personal story and makes it dramatic. So put the

✗ Drama is extreme conflict.
✗ Robert Ludlum (Borne Identity) said that he started as an actor and this carried over into his writing because his first goal is to entertain.

screenplay about your recent divorce or latest love affair back in your drawer. Instead write a story that will be a positive experience for you and one which will evoke strong emotional responses from your audience, who will identify with your characters and your story.

BLUEPRINT FOR SCREENWRITING

1. Which stories do you feel passionate about writing? Why you feel this way?
2. Write a couple of pages to answer the question "Why I Write?"
3. Can you be objective about your work? If you can't, write about why?
4. Are you writing about something that just happened? Are you too EMOTIONALLY close to the subject? Does it hurt too much when you write about it?
5. Do you feel excited enough about your story to work on it for six months to a year? If the answer is yes, what are the reasons you feel this way?
6. What are your motives for writing this story? Are you wanting to share your beliefs with others? Do you have something philosophical to say? Do you have a moral or ethic you feel strongly about? Explain.

Chapter 3

Constructing Your Blueprint: Laying Down the Framework

"I always begin with a character, or characters and then try to think up as much action for them as possible."

—John Irving

CHARACTER IS ACTION; ACTION IS CHARACTER

"Should I develop a character first and then a story, or should I develop a story first and then create a character?" "Is the plot more important than the Character or is the Character more important than the plot?"

These are questions many beginning writers ask when they first start their screenplay. However, there isn't really an answer because you don't develop either one first and the other second. Story and character develop from each other. They are synergistic and each one emanates from the other. Why? Each one is dependent on the other, because the character is the action and the action is the character. They are one and the same.

What does this mean? Let's look and see. Do you remember that special relative you always loved and admired? Do you ever wonder what happened to the mysterious couple who lived in your neighborhood and always had their shades drawn? Do you still fantasize about the most handsome guy in your high school? The one you had a crush on and who didn't know you existed? *Character drives plot*

In all of the above examples you had a particular person in mind, someone you knew, liked or feared. If you decided to write about any one of these people you would end up with a character, but you wouldn't have a plot. It would then be your job to take the character and put him in an exciting story. As you would get to know your character you'd begin to create the proper environment, problems and conflicts for him or her. Your story would develop as your character would develop. You would lay out your plot according to your character's choices, his or her decisions, actions and reactions. In other words the person your character is and what he or she does determines the plot structure of your screenplay. *Character driven films*

Character driven films are those in which the focus is on the character rather than the action. Such examples of classic character driven films are _Tootsie_, or _Rocky_. In both cases, each screenplay features, and is named for, the main character. Each script also illustrates how the main character determines the action. You'd never create a frail, slight, educated character to play the role of Rocky. Nor would you create a stocky, muscle-bound character to play the role of Tootsie, who impersonates a woman in order to get a lead as a woman in a television soap opera. Could you imagine Mike Myers playing the role of Rocky or an action hero like Harrison Ford playing the role of Tootsie? Of course you wouldn't, because these characters wouldn't be realistic or create the necessary action to make the screenplays work.

Who your character is, what he thinks, feels and believes will determine how he or she will behave. Your character's actions must be consistent with his or her personality. You must have your character be realistic and believable through his or her inner motivation, desires, drives, as well as his or her outer goal. This will be discussed more in depth in a later chapter.

Starting With a Topic or an Issue

(handwritten: (Subject) or Subject)

On the other hand, let's suppose you always have been interested in subjects such as World War II or fire fighters. These subjects always intrigued you and you've decided you want to write a script featuring one of these topics. You'd then need to create characters who would relate to the subject you chose and who'd motivate the proper action for your script. *(handwritten: Subject Driven Films)*

Whether or not you choose a character for your subject or a subject for your character, you then must create a story that is exciting and dramatic for your structure. Some examples of the subject type films are *Saving Private Ryan* to illustrate World War II. For the subject of fires and the fire-fighters who put them out, a great example is *Backdraft*. *(handwritten: Issue Driven Films)*

If you can't come up with an interesting subject or a fascinating character, what do you write about? Well, what are your beliefs, your opinions and feelings about specific social issues confronting you in the world. They could be such world issues as being against toxic waste or child abuse. These are just a few examples of broad topics that you could write about that would interest your audience. But an issue is not enough to write about. In each case you would need to create a character and a story to dramatize your point-of-view about the issue. Movies of this nature are: *The Insider*, *Mystic River*, or *Erin Brockovich*.

It really doesn't matter how you get your idea for a screenplay. What does matter is that you care about what you write. For me, the most successful stories are those small personal ones about the average man or woman. Stories about people who want what you and I want, who feel what you and I feel, are the ones with whom your audience can identify.

(handwritten: Emotion Driven)

Emotional relationships between people make the most powerfully moving stories. Stories that involve personal struggles have the most impact. Stories about lovers, families, friends, and enemies, are those that are universal and touch everyone. They deal with the powerful emotions of love, hate, joy, sorrow, anger, jealously and fear. This is the stuff from which great films and novels are created. Examples of these types of are *The Ice Storm*, *Good Will Hunting*, and *American Beauty*. These works make you laugh and cry, but most of

(handwritten: Chasing Amy)

[handwritten margin note: DID YOU MAKE THEM FEEL SOME- THING FOR EACH SCENE?]

all they make you FEEL. They move you just the way they moved the person who wrote them. They were written by people who really cared and in turn, made the audience really care.

As you think about your writing take the raw materials buried inside you and start to mine them. Discover the human element of your story and make it personal. By doing this your writing will become universal and everyone who sees your screenplay will be emotionally involved.

Laying Down the Framework

"I don't see how anybody starts a movie without knowing how it's going to end."

—John Barth

By now you've chosen the character, subject or issue you want to write about. But you probably aren't certain what to do next. Well, the next thing you are to do is nothing. That's right. Live with your idea for a while. Think about it 24 hours a day. Let it germinate. Mull it over, sleep with it, visualize it before you commit any words to paper. It is important for you to look at all aspects of your idea and explore all the different possibilities opened to you before you begin your blueprint.

If you give your story idea enough time to incubate, a story structure will eventually begin to appear. By thinking about your story it will begin to take a shape. But in order to have your vague idea become a well-structured story, you must do more than think about it. You now need to deal with the craft of structuring your story. This entails organizing your time, thoughts, and ideas. It requires discipline to develop the proper story structure you'll need so your writing won't collapse.

Now, you must lay down a framework as the foundation on which to build the entire structure of your screenplay. Earlier, I compared a writer constructing a blueprint for screenwriting to an architect constructing a blueprint for a home. For instance, let's say you hired an architect to build you a home. Well, she first must know the type of STRUCTURE you want and then she must draw up a set of plans. A blueprint. However, the architect can't do this until you give her pertinent information about the style you prefer. Do you want a California Ranch or an English Tudor? Maybe you want a two story Colonial complete with columns. Or do you prefer Spanish Modern?

Your architect needs to know what type of home before laying down the framework for the desired end result for your house. Whatever style you choose will determine the measurements and specifications of the framework from the blueprint which will shape your house. The framework is the skeleton of your home and without the framework your house would collapse.

The exact same process happens when you start to structure your screenplay. You must first create your blueprint and lay down the framework. You need to determine your characters, the plot, the conflicts, and most important of all—how your story opens and how it ends. That is considered the framework for your screenplay.

I guarantee you it's much easier to create a blueprint to follow as a guide or direction for your story, then it is to write a screenplay without one. Writers who resist developing an blueprint, often think it stops their creative flow or takes too much time and energy to prepare. Can you image an architect trying to build a house without first developing a blueprint? It would end in chaos.

The same is true for you writers. You'll eventually end up wasting your time and sapping all your creative energy. Not creating a blueprint is a pretty difficult way to write, because the writing often becomes disjointed and without focus. It's much easier to lay down your framework before you start your script.

From Fade In to Fade Out

It's important to decide what type of screenplay you plan to write and then layout the blueprint and the framework from Fade In to Fade Out. The opening and the ending are your parameters to follow so you won't turn a comedy into a tragedy half-way through your screenplay. When you write without a blueprint your screenplay doesn't have a solid structure.

You'll want to construct your basic structure and build your framework so your story won't collapse in the middle. How do you do this? You do this by knowing how your screenplay ends and then working backwards to find the opening for it. The "Fade In" that starts your script and the "Fade Out" that ends your script is your framework.

Knowing your ending gives you destination to follow and your characters a path to reach. Can you imagine trying to get from Los Angeles to Manhattan or Seattle without a road map? Well, that's what you do when you write without a blueprint. It's like taking a trip without a map—and leads nowhere except to a dead end. If you don't have a direction for your characters or you don't know how you're going to resolve your story, you will be heading for major detours and probably get lost along the way. Even if you change your ending over and over again, you at least need to have one when you begin your screenplay.

Once you have decided on your ending you then have a destination for all of your scenes that build up to the climax. There are many people who say they don't know the ending when they start to write and just let their characters take them where they want to go. Let me assure you these writers and their characters are heading for disaster.

Would you go to the airport and get on a plane without knowing your destination? You could end up in Russia or South America. Would you get on a ship and just let it go wherever the current took it? I hardly think so. You certainly would have your destination determined before you embarked for your trip.

Well, the same is true for writing your screenplay. You have to know where you want to go and what direction to follow, and every scene you write must lead to that destination.

STORY STRUCTURE

After you've determined your ending and your opening you still have to fill over a hundred or more pages in between. Perhaps your story is not clear and your characters are still vague. Maybe you don't have any idea what you are to do next.

Ask yourself, "What is my story about?" Next, try to tell your LOGLINE story in a couple of sentences. The two or three sentences you use to tell your story will become your plot structure or the premise of your screenplay. Every scene you write will have to relate to these couple of sentences. They will become the story structure from which you'll layout your screenplay.

When you look in the movie section of your newspaper or read the TV Guide to find out what a television movie is about, you are reading the log line or the plot structure of the films. When you begin you must be able to do the same thing, to reduce your entire story to two or three sentences, as in the movie section of the newspaper or the TV Guide. If you can't write your story idea in a concise and succinct manner, you probably don't have the right structure.

Beginning Relates to the Ending

Now that you've determined where and when you'll open your story you have to know that in a well-structured screenplay the beginning should always relate to the end. What do I mean by that statement? Let's suppose you want to write a murder mystery. Before you start your story you must know how it is going to end. You need to decide in advance if you'll have the murderer caught or if you'll have him escape in the end. Will he be arrested, convicted, sent to prison, flee to another country or be killed? As you can see, until you know the ending you won't be able to write a single word. How can you possibly plant the necessary clues or foreshadow events to solve your story if you don't know in advance how it will end? How can your characters be properly motivated to behave in a realistic manner? How can you set up red herrings or twists and turns for your plot if you don't know how the mystery ends?

You can't. Many writers have avoided trying to know the ending in advance and they usually ended up with an illogical plot. To further illustrate this point, let's suppose you have a young woman killed in the opening of your story. If you decide in advance that by the end her boyfriend has an air-tight alibi and is innocent, your story would be completely different than if in the ending he was apprehended and confessed to the crime.

If you had a story where you wanted the boyfriend to be guilty, but never caught, then in the end, you might show him being with a beautiful woman sipping exotic drinks in a foreign country. Al-

though the opening is the same in all examples, your ending will determine the direction the entire story and your characters will take.

Successful screenplays have a definite structure and all the
scenes lead to the climax and resolution of the plot. That's why it's
important for you to know your ending FIRST. Once you have your
ending then ask yourself, "Where do I open my story?" "What will
be the best opening I can have?"

In developing your opening you must do several things. You need
to introduce your main character of your screenplay, reveal the
problem or mystery that must be solved, and ask the dramatic question that must be answered. Your opening will only make sense if it
relates to the ending. In other words it's really impossible for you to
know where to open your story unless you have some idea of how
you want it to end. Of course, the ending might change many times,
but at least you need an arbitrary ending so the seeds of it will be
planted in the opening. By doing this you'll enable your main character to have an immediate goal he or she must reach. The opening
which needs to be dramatic rather than static immediately begins
the action of your story. *A SEARCH FOR REASONS TO CONTINUE READING*

A screenplay or a television movie is really nothing more than a
search for reasons. You state the problem in the opening scene and
then search for reasons to develop it throughout the entire script
until you solve it in the climax. In your opening something must immediately happen to set off your story and to capture your audience's interest.

Hooking the Audience

You must hook or grab your audience in the first few minutes. What
I mean by "hooking your audience" is to get their attention immediately. In the television industry there are many competing networks,
cable stations and independents vying for viewers. If you can grab
your viewers' attention and hold it through commercials until your
movie is over you will have written a good script. *TEASER OR HOOK*

That is the reason you often see an exciting scene taken from the
middle of a television movie and shown out of sequence before the
movie begins. This is known as a "Teaser" or the "Hook." It is shown
so as to grab the viewers so they'll continue to watch. For example, if

the movie is about a detective, the teaser might show a chase scene or a crime being committed. This gets the viewers interested immediately. Hopefully, they'll be hooked! It takes the best type of writing to accomplish this feat.

In motion pictures you want to hold your audience's attention from the opening credits until "The End" flashes on the screen. You want to keep them in the theater, so they won't leave, or worse yet, ask for their money back. One way of accomplishing this goal is to ask yourself when you open your screenplay the following question: "Why is this day different from any other day?" "What happens at the onset of my story that is going to set-off the entire action of my structure?"

Expl.

A. I.

In the opening of *A.I.* a little boy, David, is the product of a company which built him. He is called a "mecha" and is a robot, who is also created to experience love. He's adopted by an employee of the company and his distraught wife, because their son is in a comatose state. David is getting to know his parents and beginning to have feelings for them when suddenly he has to go out on his own when his adopted parents' son recovers. The dramatic question which sets off the story in film is: What will happen to David when he is thrust out into the world alone?

The reason an opening is so important is that it draws in your audience to your story. If they had never seen David getting to like living with his adoptive parents and rooting for the relationship to work, they wouldn't be emotional when he's told to leave. They wouldn't care. However, because the audience is involved with David they now worry about what will his fate be. What will become of him? Will he survive? Will he get hurt? Will he find other parents? These are the questions the audience are watching to see if they are answered during the course of the film.

Your audience must understand what the movie they are going to see is about. They must be interested enough to keep wanting to watch it through to its conclusion. For some reason a lot of writers like to keep their audience in the dark. This doesn't work and is a sure-fire way to lose your audience. It's important to immediately involve your viewers and bring them into the world of which you're writing. Your audience must have a sense of who the players are and what the rules are of this new world. You want to immediately get your audience to identify with your characters and their plight.

Expl.

If you've decided to write a romantic love story, you must first decide if the couple will get together in the end or break up. After you know your ending, you must relate your opening to it. Think of the wonderful romantic feature films of the 1940s and 1950s, the ones with Spencer Tracy and Kathryn Hepburn, or Rock Hudson and Doris Day. They followed a usual formula. Boy meets girl in the opening. Boy loses girl somewhere in the middle. Boy gets girl in the end. The beginning always relates to the ending

In the opening of *The Royal Tenenbaums,* the estranged father played by Gene Hackman wants to reconcile with his family, and so he tells them he's terminally ill. This event sets off the story. But the story is really about healing the relationships between the father and his children. Will they finally be able to have a positive relationships? Will the children be able to get over their resentment towards their father abandoning them? This is the dramatic question that will be answered in the end of the story.

Now that you've learned the importance of constructing the framework of your story, you are well on your way to developing the rest of your Blueprint for Screenwriting. You have the ending that gives your story its direction, and the opening that sets off your screenplay. You're now on the road to steer your story in the right direction, create a complex character with a goal, and develop a blueprint to follow so you'll know where you're going, how to get there and when you've arrived.

BLUEPRINT FOR SCREENWRITING

1. Find the ending of your story and write it in a paragraph in present tense prose.
2. After you write the ending find the proper opening of your story. Write the opening in a paragraph in present tense prose with the character's goal in the opening. What is the dramatic question you need to answer throughout the script?
3. Does your beginning relate to your ending? How?
4. Create your blueprint for writing, so you have a direction to follow on your writing journey.

Chapter 4

Story Structure:
The Screenplay's
Foundation

"A writer's material is what he cares about."

—John Gardner

That you care about.

The foundation of your screenplay will be solid and secure and won't collapse if you build a strong structure. By now you have determined how your story will end and how it will begin. In your opening, the main character has been introduced with a specific problem to solve, or a dramatic question to answer. This allows you to set up the goal which your main character has to reach in the climax. For example, in the movie *Schindler's List*, Oskar Schindler's goal during the Holocaust is to save as many Jews as he possibly can from certain death in the gas chamber, by employing them to work for him in his factory.

In a romantic comedy adapted from Helen Fielding's popular novel of the same name, *Bridget Jones's Diary*, Bridget, slightly overweight, in her thirties and insecure, desperately falls in love with her boss, Daniel, a charming and dashing man.

31

Bridget's desperate goal is to have a romantic relationship with him, which ends up disappointing for her, when she discovers him cheating with another woman. Devastated, she begins to see Mark, a quiet and shy man. Eventually Daniel wants her back and this creates a three-way love triangle. The dramatic question of the screenplay is will Bridget choose the right man as her lover?

Expl.

In another romantic comedy, *Sleepless in Seattle*, the goal of the main character, Annie, is to find Sam, a widower who lives on the other side of the country in Seattle. After she listens to his son's plea on the radio to find a wife for his father, she becomes truly motivated to finding this adorable boy and his father. Annie's desperate goal is to meet Sam, with whom she believes she loves and is the woman destined to be with him and his son.

In both *Bridget Jones's Diary* and *Sleepless in Seattle* the main character has a desperate goal, not only for love, but love for a *specific character* and the hopes it will be reciprocated. If you write about your characters wanting love it must be directed to a specific character and not used as looking for love in the abstract.

In a script, your audience must be hooked by the first five to ten minutes or the first five to ten pages of your screenplay. They must be involved with your main character and his or her immediate goal. If you don't succeed in hooking your audience at once your story will have failed, because your audience won't have anyone to root for.

HAVE A DESPERATE GOAL

Your main character must always have a goal he or she desperately wants to reach. By giving the main character a desperate goal to reach you'll get your audience's interest, and hold it until the end of your film.

BEING FLEXIBLE WHEN BUILDING YOUR BLUEPRINT

You begin to develop a solid foundation of your script by first developing your structure in an arbitrary manner, so you will be able and willing to give up parts of your story that don't work. It's important not to commit yourself to any particular idea or character in a rigid manner. You must build your structure carefully and slowly, letting it develop into a solid foundation step by step.

You'd be amazed at the resistance writers have against making changes in their writing, after they've written their script. In my workshops there are students who will argue, become defensive, and even a few who never finish what they start, because they can't be objective. You could say they have tunnel vision and can only see their story from a one-dimensional perspective. This is not a good trait to have when you are trying to structure your story. Writers who are successful shaping a solid structure are those willing to make changes over and over again.

In other words, you must be flexible. This trait is probably the most important one all writers should have. If you find yourself being rigid about your writing it's important that you learn to be able to give up those areas in your writing that don't work. To be flexible you also must be willing to add characters or scenes that you need to make your story work.

Being flexible allows you to create your work as an artist would create a piece of sculpture. The writer like the sculptor must be flexible. In sculpting, your medium may be clay, which is malleable. If you are sculpting a human figure, you look at the entire body to see the overall structure. You might begin with the face and move to the trunk or the arm, always sculpting the parts in relationship to their overall structure. When you make a change in one area it effects the entire work. Be aware of the relationship of the sum to all the parts when you are structuring your writing. After you begin your story, think of it as if you are working with clay and be flexible when you make changes to look at the over-all structure so it won't collapse.

The Climax Must Have Closure

With this in mind, let's talk about the climax of your story. The climax is the highest point of drama in your structure. It is where all of the scenes must lead throughout your story. Finding the ending of your story is the first thing to do. The ending of your screenplay is known as the climax. After the climax your story should be finished and can't go any further. Your screenplay is complete and if you keep writing then your writing becomes anticlimactic, which means you've written too much and you have no resolution for your screenplay. Your audience should leave your movie feeling emotionally satisfied. If your audience doesn't have a sense of closure in the climax your script is a failure. CLOSURE

What is the purpose for writing anything if you have nothing to say as a writer? There is no purpose. What is writing all about if it's not to share your viewpoint, your passion or your personal vision of life, death, love, birth, relationships and yourself?

When you write about a subject that has meaning to you and is important, unconsciously your message will come through in the characters and the story. That's what I mean when I tell you to write about something that's important to you, about which you care. It will give your writing a much deeper level, especially if your audience goes away intrigued with or at least provoked by your idea or point-of-view of the world.

I can't stress the importance of finding the right climax. You'll probably have to change your climax many times before it works. Some writers have written an entire screenplay before they discovered the climax wasn't working and it had to be written over again. This is not uncommon, so don't get discouraged, because once you find the right climax you'll be satisfied and your story will make sense.

In order to determine your climax you must be sure to include the three important elements in it. The most important element in the climax is the main character must experience a change. He or she must reach a new understanding and discover something about him or herself or another character that he or she didn't know before. In psychological terms he or she would experience a catharsis and gain some new insight about him or herself. If your main character doesn't change or experience an emotional transformation then your climax will fail.

Your Intention Is Your Theme

The final element that occurs in the climax is your theme is revealed. Your reason for writing this particular story is made known through your main character. Perhaps you're against abortion, capital punishment, or divorce. It's not necessary in the beginning to state: "My personal vision of life is _____." However, if you care about an issue in your script your point-of-view about it will be revealed in the climax.

For example, in *Shawshank Redemption*, the theme is about an innocent man, Andrew Dufresne, played by Tim Robbins, who is in a drab and dreary prison in Ohio. His goal is to escape and he uses his wit and brains to achieve this end. In the end the audience goes from feeling hopeless to feeling hopeful and experiences a catharsis as Andrew is on the path of freedom for a new life.

Expl.

In the film *The Insider*, based on the real life scientist, Jeffrey Wigand, played by Russell Crowe, he is upset when he discovers that tobacco companies are manipulating the drug in their product to deliberately get people addicted. He decides to become a whistle blower after he discovers what harm the company is causing to people who smoke. He gets fired from B&W corporation for taking a stand. His goal is to reveal the truth of the tobacco industry against all odds, including the betrayal of the producers of the television show *60 Minutes* who decided not to run the interview with him, when they're threatened with a lawsuit by Brown and Williamson. This excellent screenplay is exciting and suspenseful, but more so because of the theme of the little guy fighting a Goliath corporation and how he doesn't give up in the face of threats and betrayals.

The Spine of Your Story

After you've determined what will happen to your main character in the climax and how your story will open in relationship to the climax, you really have the plot structure or spine of your story. This is the skeleton that holds your entire foundation together. The spine of your story is your structure that goes in a straight line from the opening to the climax.

SPINE

Imagine an old fashioned clothesline which you're hanging your clothes on so they'll dry. Now visualize every scene you write as being attached to the spine of your story like each item of clothing is attached to a clothesline. Without the spine or structure you have no story, just unconnected scenes which become episodic. You need to understand the importance of finding the spine of your screenplay. It is the foundation of your well-structured writing.

After you find your story structure, you need to tell your story in a couple of sentences, as I discussed in the previous chapter. These sentences will become known as your story structure, which will give your script focus. As you start to write your story you will then relate each scene you write to this story structure by asking yourself if the scene you're about to write is connected to it.

Sometimes these few sentences are called your premise, your plot structure or your logline. You then write all the scenes directly related to these few sentences.

Here is an example of a logline from a recently completed screenplay that I co-wrote with Brenda Krantz.

Logline or Story Structure

Expl,

> While trying to breed the violence out of Killer Bees, an experimental misbreeding with a livestock Botfly leads to disaster for the Scientist and the small farming town. Josh Fielding, his young lab assistant and his four teen-aged friends are desperate to stop these cunning killers as they destroy everything in their path. No one is safe as Josh and his friends soon discover—with tragic results.

In a screenplay, if a scene doesn't relate to your story structure, you don't need it in your script and must remove it, even if it's one of your best scenes. Remember your script can only have one storyline. This prevents it from becoming fragmented or disjointed. You are telling your story from the point-of-view of the main character. Your story structure must be written in a direct line from the opening to the climax.

Causal Writing

As I said earlier, the biggest problem I have found with the beginning writer, and even with the most experienced professional, is that the writing is usually episodic. This means that the scenes don't relate to one another and the screenplay doesn't have the underlying story structure that sets off the story and keeps it moving until the resolution or end. From fade in to fade out your structure must not collapse in the middle or your entire script won't work.

The beginning of your story should relate to the end in a causal manner. What I mean is, there has to be a connection between the beginning scene right through to the final scene of your screenplay. If there is no connection then there is no structure, and you are only writing episodic writing. Episodic writing is not connected by a structure, and each scene usually has no relationship to the next one. In an anthology the stories aren't connected. In *Arabian Nights*, the stories are episodic and not connected to one another.

In a screenplay, all scenes must be connected to one another from the opening scene through to as many as fifty or more scenes. How can you learn to do this? By planning your ending first and then working backwards to your opening. Your opening scene must lead to the next scene which motivates the following scene. Just as Toni Morrison wrote: "Always know the ending; that's where I start."

The ending is the beginning.

BLUEPRINT FOR SCREENWRITING

1. Describe your main character's goal in a couple of sentences. Is it clear and specific?
2. How does the main character change or discover something he didn't know before in the climax?
3. How is your plot resolved in the climax?
4. What is the theme of your screenplay and how do you reveal your theme in the climax?
5. In the climax of your screenplay you need to find the answer to the following questions: "Does the main character grow and change in the climax?" "Is the plot of my screenplay resolved in the climax?" "Am I successful in getting my vision across in the climax?"

If you answered "yes" to all these questions you are well on your way of building a solid story structure as the foundation for your screenplay.

Chapter 5

The Main Character

"You can never know enough about your characters."
—Somerset Maugham

The next step of your writing journey toward writing a completed, exciting screenplay is to focus on the main character or protagonist. To create a successful main character takes hard work and a lot of thought. A character just doesn't happen. A character is born through the labor of your imagination, investigation, and examination. All this work eventually culminates in developing a believable, complex character.

When I first began teaching at UCLA Writer's Program, I discovered that creating characters was (and still is) the biggest problem for most writers. Even in stories that were well-structured, the weakest link was always the characters. Some were clichéd, others one-dimensional, many were weak and others were boring. No matter how great the story if the characters were stock or stereotypical the screenplay flopped. In this chapter you'll learn the techniques for developing an original main character who makes your screenplay work.

To create a fascinating and compelling major characters you'll have to start the journey to delve into your own self. After all, you

39

are the creator of a world, which is peopled with many different human beings. You're the one who develops all the characters and it is up to you whether or not they'll be unique, memorable and original.

Therefore, before you begin to write your screenplay you have to decide who your main character will be. Although it is true that you'll have many characters in your script, in order to have a direction or focus for your screenplay you may only have one main character, hero or protagonist in your story. This is an important rule to remember. For example, when you go on a journey you can only reach one destination at a time. You can't possibly be in two different places at the same time. How can you be in New York and Los Angeles at the very exact moment? You can't.

THE MAIN CHARACTER'S JOURNEY

Well, the same is also true for your main character. You can only follow one character's journey in your screenplay at one time. Of course, you may have many characters in your screenplay, but you only have one main character to follow in your screenplay. If you try to follow more than one character's point-of-view, your screenplay will become unfocused and confusing.

Many beginning writers start their screenplay without knowing who the main character is and their writing isn't focused because of that reason. However, there are several ways to determine your main character. Ask yourself these following questions to discover who your main character will be in your screenplay.

"Does my main character have a specific goal that he desperately wants to achieve?"

"Is my main character active and not passive throughout the story?"

"Does my main character change or transform in the climax?"

If the answers to all the questions are "yes," then you've chosen the right main character.

I'm certain you can recall a few movies which seem to have more than one main character. It's always inevitable in my classes that someone will point out the exceptions to this rule. When the students and I discuss the rule of having only one main character there are invariably a few students who will challenge it.

"What about *When Harry Met Sally*?" "What about *Romeo and Juliet*?"

In each case there is still only one main character. Based on the above questions you were instructed to ask yourself, can you guess which one is the main character in each story?

If you answered Harry and Romeo as the main characters in each story you made the right choices. Why? Because Harry and Romeo are the characters who have a specific goal which moves the story forward. For instance, in the case of Harry in *When Harry Met Sally*, he's the one of the two who creates the driving force that moves the story toward a specific goal, which is having a love affair.

To get better acquainted with your characters you need to delve into their past, just like you did with yourself, to discover how they became who they are in your screenplay. Since a character's actions must develop from the kind of person he is, you really can't begin your story until your have a thorough understanding of what makes your characters tick.

THE CHARACTER BIOGRAPHY

You develop knowledge of your characters through in-depth scrutiny of them by creating their past life. You accomplish this by creating a character biography for your main character and all major characters. A character biography is exactly what it says—a personal history and inventory of your character's traits, make-up and personality. *Def,*

A character biography enables you to create a backstory for your characters and give them memories and life experiences from their past. After all, your characters don't exist in a void. They exist in your screenplay in the present, but come from a context in the past with a rich personal history. There are three categories for the character biography. They are the Social, the Physical and the Emotional aspects of your character. As you develop each category you'll get to know your characters inside out. Let's start with the physical.

The Physical BIOGRAPHY

The physical aspects of your character are rather basic. They include his or her height, weight, hair color, eye color, how he or she walks, talks, eats, smiles, body language, mannerisms, gestures, posture. What is his over-all appearance? Is he handsome, ugly, weak, strong, stocky, fat, thin?

Don't just arbitrarily give your characters physical characteristics without first knowing their character. Certainly, the character "Rocky" could never have been a frail-looking, thin, studious type. If he were, the movie *Rocky* would have been a different movie.

The character determines the action, but the action also comes from the character. It's amazing how a person's appearance affects the way he feels about himself and how he behaves. Think about the type of character you physically need for your story and then develop him so he's realistic and authentic in his physical make-up.

A beautiful woman is treated differently from an unattractive one. A muscular, tall man gets more attention from the opposite sex than and out-of-shape, overweight man.

The Social Biography

The social aspects of your character involve everything that deals with his social world and his place in society. This includes his education: is he a drop-out or is he highly educated? Besides education, the social aspects are economic status, religion, race, politics, family environment, friends, work, avocation, and vocation. It includes taste in music, food, plays, sports, liquor, literature, art, and all outside interests.

What does she do with her leisure time? How does she spend her vacations? Is she upper-class or lower-class? Is she an intellectual or is she illiterate?

The importance of knowing your character's place or social standing in relation to society is obvious. How she sees herself and how others view her are based in a large part on her social and economic position in society.

The Emotional Biography (beneath the mask)

To me, this category is the most important. Knowing the physical and social characteristics of a person enables you to know him only in a superficial way. But discovering the emotional life of your character helps you learn about the person beneath the smile or mask.

And isn't that what writing is all about? You want to unpeel the layers of protective covering that hides the real person inside. And you
do this by putting your character under stress, tension and pressure.
Become aware of your own emotions and ask yourself, "What would
I feel in the same situation?"

By answering this question before you write you'll be using yourself as the most potent emotional resource of all.

The emotional life of your character will determine how he'll act
and react in a stressful situation. If a person is insecure he will behave different from a confident person in the same situation. Until
you can understand the emotional make-up of your character, you
won't be able to develop the proper motivation for his behavior.
Some of the emotional aspects of your character could include his
self-esteem. Does he feel confident about himself? Is she unsure of
herself? What are his dreams, his hopes, his fears, his loves, his fantasies, his aspirations, his joys, his pain? Is she an extrovert, intro-
vert, cautious, fool-hardy, boisterous?

THE MAIN CHARACTER'S MOTIVATION

After you've completed your character biography for all the important characters, you will be in a position to plan your story with the
proper motivation for all your characters in order to make them realistic. Motivation drives your character, creates your character's
point-of-view, and is the basis for the character's emotional growth
and transformation. You'll be able to motivate your character's behavior in a manner consistent with his personality when you find
answers to his inner motives.

One of the biggest problems with characterization is many of you
don't know how to motivate your character's behavior. If you don't
lay down the reasons for their actions, they will be implausible, in-
consistent or unbelievable. This is the main reason characters become stilted, unreal, and contrived in your script.

Here are two important questions you need to answer to discover
your main character's motivation within your story structure:

What does my main character desperately want? *1.*

What motivates my main character to change in the climax? *2.*

Does this sound simple? Well, it's not. If you are thoroughly able to answer these questions you have the blueprint for your main character. Most importantly you have begun your journey to discover your main character's inner and outer journey.

Example of Character Motivation: A Case Study

In my writing workshops, I always have the class develop a character biography for the protagonist and the antagonist. Here's an example of creating character motivation and back story for them.

In this example, I gave the entire class a husband and wife who are living in a bad relationship and they were to create a story for this couple, including their backstory.

At first they tried to develop a story, but they kept getting stuck. They finally realized it's impossible to create a story until they knew who the main character was and how the story would end. After they had decided whether the main character would be the husband or the wife, they then had to write character biographies for each character to motivate their actions. The students soon learned the importance of a character biography, because they've discovered they can't develop the story until they know their characters.

Let's suppose the husband and wife are having marital problems. The first thing the class must decide is which character to make the main character. Let's suppose they decide to make the woman the main character. By establishing the woman as the main character the class immediately knows the story will be told from her point-of-view. She will be the one to struggle toward a specific goal. And in the end she will be the one who changes and experiences an emotional transformation.

Expl.
EMOTIONAL
CHANGE

The class decided the woman's emotional pole-to-pole development would be from dependent to independent. This would give the main character an emotional structure which had to be consistent throughout the work.

Now the class had the ending, the main character, and the emotional change. Next, they had to create a goal to give the main character a vehicle to struggle toward.

Since character is story and story is character the class couldn't develop one without developing the other. They couldn't create the story and fit the character into it anymore than they could create a character to fit a plot.

The class soon discovered that the process of writing was to develop motivation for the character by asking the most important question, "WHY?" For every "Why" they asked, they had to find the right answer in order to get the character's actions properly motivated. And if they changed one aspect of the character they had to make changes in all the characters, since each character affects the other.

They also learned that in the same set of circumstances the story could be completely different, depending on the character traits of the main character. For example, if the wife is in her middle 40s and has been married practically all of her adult life, her behavior would be different from a married woman in her late 20s who has her own identity and career apart from her marriage. If each woman discovers her husband is having an affair, their reactions and actions would be based on who they are. The older woman might be afraid to be alone and might forgive him, trading her pride for financial security. The younger woman might leave her husband, since she has her own career and is already independent.

The class decided to make the main character the older woman and have her discover her husband's infidelity in the opening of the story. The next thing they did was start to delve inside the character by asking questions: "What will she do now?" "How do we motivate her to go from dependent to independent during the course of the story?" "Why would she tolerate such outrageous behavior on the part of her husband?" "What kind of woman is she?"

Besides doing an extensive character biography on her, the class also had to discover what her past life experiences were. Where did she come from? Why did she behave the way she did? What was her childhood like? They had to answer all these questions. Knowing them would give the main character a back story or past to draw from.

After a lot of discussion, they decided she had to be very dependent upon her husband because she got married right after high school. She grew up in the 1950s when a woman's acculturation was to be a wife and mother. Since she has been busy with raising their three children, she and her husband have grown apart. He has been developing his professional career as a business executive and spending most of his time away from home.

Her purpose in life was her home and children. Now, the children are grown and the last one has just left home for college. In fact, she was just returning from taking her child to his new university, when she came home and found her husband with another woman. Of course, she is devastated, because she loves her husband and desperately wants the marriage to work. He is all she has ever known and up until this moment he's all she ever wanted.

Her husband makes some feeble excuse and promises her it will never happen again. He tells her it was just one of those foolish things that sometimes happen to executives and their young, attractive co-workers, but it doesn't mean a thing. The wife wants to believe him and finally forgives him. But underneath, deep in her subconscious, something begins to gnaw at her. The tinge of doubt. Somewhere in her secret heart of hearts she doesn't believe her husband. Although it is still not conscious, she gets a slight awareness that things haven't been right in her marriage for a long time. But consciously she tells herself things will work out.

The two maintain the appearance of a happy marriage on the outside, but inside, our main character is slowly beginning to change. She slowly begins to realize what her marriage is really like, without having the children at home to act as a buffer, between her and her husband.

On the surface she does everything to make the marriage pleasant. But underneath the surface she's been burned, and the pain is changing her. She slowly takes small steps to change her life. She begins by taking an art class at a community college. She has always been artistically inclined, decorating her home and her husband's office. She was always the parent who created the art posters for her children's classes at school.

At first she is nervous about going back to school after all these years. But she soon discovers her artistic talent is admired and respected by her teacher, a young man in his early 30s. She is flattered. It's been a long time since she has done something for herself. With her teacher's encouragement, she eventually gets enough confidence to matriculate to get her fine-arts degree.

Her husband objects. Being a full-time student will take her away from her homemaking duties. But there is a change in our main character. She doesn't listen to her husband! For the first time in years she is feeling some self-worth and says she's going to get her degree. She is scared, but she feels a new sense of self-respect. She begins to develop an idea of who she is, apart from her role of wife and mother. Through hard work she soon discovers she is not only talented, but also intelligent.

She struggles with her classes and art projects and she receives an award in the college art show. She soon gets requests for her art and even sells a few of her paintings. Her first teacher, the young man who encouraged her, and she have become very close. He would like an intimate relationship with her, but she realizes she doesn't want to go from one man to another—that is not the answer.

In the end she discovers she wants to make it on her own, because she is no longer the dependent, desperate woman she was in the beginning. (The beginning relates to the end.) In the climactic scene she tells her husband, to his dismay, she no longer wants to be married to him and asks him for a divorce.

Our main character's transformation arc developed from dependent to independent. Her discovery or change in the climax is that she realizes she doesn't need to live through a man. She won't compromise herself anymore just to stay married. In the end we have a changed woman who has struggled for and finally attained, self-respect and a sense of independence. At least in the end she is going to try to make it on her own, which is something she wouldn't even try in the beginning of the story.

This class exercise always proves invaluable to the students. Through doing this exercise they begin to learn the process of character development and motivation. Try doing this exercise for your own story. Work with your characters and develop the necessary past and present life history for them. Build a solid foundation for your characters, so they won't fall apart and collapse halfway through your work. You'll discover that your screenplay will intrigue your audience, when you make your characters realistic human beings.

BLUEPRINT FOR WRITING

1. Write an extensive character biography for your main and major characters. Include:
   (a) Social
   (b) Emotional
   (c) Physical
2. Have you properly motivated each character?
3. Is your character behaving consistently throughout your story?
4. Create a past or case history for your main character.
5. How does your character's past, influence his or her behavior in the present? Explain in detail.
6. What is the main character's emotional pole-to-pole change? Example: From dependence to independence
   free independence p. 44

Chapter 6

Characters and Conflict

> "The gem cannot be polished without friction, nor man perfected without trials."
>
> —Confucius

Character conflict is the heart of drama for your screenplay. Your characters' emotional conflicts are what give heart and spirit to your script. It's the characters who create the conflict in your screenplay by the choices and decisions they make.

Successful screenplays are based on emotional relationships and conflicts within and among the characters. Since emotional conflict is the stuff from which great stories are made it is important for you to completely understand your character's emotional world. All characters reveal their true self under pressure, so let's look at some other important building blocks to make your blueprint for screenwriting have dramatic conflict.

CHARACTER CONFLICT

Conflict is the strength of any exciting character and story. Without conflict, characters don't have drive, desire or desperation. Without conflict there's no story, just words. Conflict is one of the most important building blocks for exciting characters and dramatic stories. Through conflict your characters shed their layers bit by bit until we discover the different aspects of their hidden self. The characters' internal conflicts create the dramatic action for your story. This chapter includes various types of conflicts and the overt and covert reactions to conflict. You'll learn how to throw characters into the middle of conflict to give them momentum, tension and suspense. It is conflict which forces them to take off their masks.

It is not enough to give your main character a specific goal he desperately wants to reach. A character must also have obstacles that stand in the way of him reaching his goal. If he doesn't have to struggle, there is no conflict, and without conflict there is no drama. Conflict is one of the major building blocks for exciting writing.

Since all dramatic writing must contain conflict, how do you get conflict? You first give your main character a goal and then you put obstacles and opposition in the path of his goal. These obstacles are necessary to create conflict. The greater the obstacles and complications, the more hurdles your main character has to overcome, the more powerful and absorbing is your conflict.

Ask yourself what would your characters fight for. What do they want desperately enough to motivate them into taking action and move the story to its climax? The ultimate question is what would your characters die for? Inherent in the answer to these questions is conflict of the best kind. The more intense the conflict the more exciting your script will be.

There are three kinds of conflict. You can use one of these types of conflict when writing your story or use all of them, which makes for more suspense and drama:

Types of Conflict

1. *Man against Himself.* Examples using this type of conflict are: *28 Days,* a story about an alcoholic; *Traffic,* about drug traffic and a politician's young teen-aged addicted daughter, and *Leaving Las Vegas,* where an alcoholic vows to drink himself to death. In each of these films the characters are trying to overcome some flaw or addiction within. Most tragedies of William Shakespeare involve this

type of conflict. Some of his most famous heroes who suffered from a tragic character flaw are Othello, Macbeth, and King Lear.

2. *Man against Nature.* This type of conflict usually deals with action-packed Adventure movies and novels such as *Alien, Planet of the Apes,* and *Twister.* The main character's goal is always thwarted by some act of nature that almost prevents him from succeeding to reach his goal. These struggles usually involve life and death issues. Will the characters survive the aliens, the apes, or the wrath of mother nature? In *Titantic* the conflict is will the largest, strongest, and solid constructed ship survive after crashing into an iceberg?

3. *Man against Man.* The main character has a goal and another character stands in the way of him reaching his goal. It is the most popular type of conflict. This conflict includes most of the mystery, spy, and war stories. But the most dramatic type of conflict with man against man is often the small personal story involving families, lovers or an important emotional relationship conflict. This type includes: *American Beauty, The Ice Storm,* and *A Beautiful Mind.*

However, in all good writing the main character and other characters should also have internal conflict, while experiencing conflicts with another character. The best conflict includes all three simultaneously. *This Boy's Life,* a wonderful coming of age film based on a memoir by Tobias Wolf, deals with a young boy in conflict with his step-father, his home environment, and with his desire to run away from his step-father. However he also wants to be with his mother and this causes him even more conflict.

This is not an example of an action-packed adventure story, but a personal story, with more conflict and punch than the greatest car crash or explosion. This film involves a young boy with internal conflicts who is limited by his choices to solve them. This is what makes the story dramatic, original and emotional.

THE SPECIFIC GOAL

A story would certainly be boring if the main character did nothing but remain passive and reactive. How do you make your main char-

acter active in your story? Give him a specific goal which he desperately wants to reach throughout the screenplay and you'll make
your main character ACTIVE. The goal determines the action. The
desperation determines the momentum and tension. This goal will
give him the proper motivation to change in the climax.

For example, in *Bend it Like Beckham*, a young girl desperately
wants to play soccer even though her parents won't allow her to,
that's her goal. In *My Best Friend's Wedding*, a young woman desperately wants to stop her former boyfriend from getting married, that's
her goal. In each case the goal is specific: to play soccer, and to keep
her boyfriend from marrying another woman.

Each main character behaves in a certain way, because of the specific goal she wants to reach. The goal moves the story forward. You
can see how the goal is the catalyst that gives your main character
the action and momentum she needs.

The specific goal also provides the character's change or transformation in the climax. In your opening, the main character immediately must be faced with a dramatic problem or question to solve,
in order to start your story moving.

"Will the detective apprehend the criminal?"

"Will the young girl's parents allow her to play soccer?"

"Will the young woman win back her old boyfriend and prevent
his marriage to another woman?"

Each one has a goal which becomes the driving force that gives the
screenplay movement, energy and a purpose. The important thing to
remember about your character's goal is that it must be specific. It
can't be abstract. You can't just say your character wants love, power
or money. These are all abstractions and are too vague a goal. If your
character wants love it must be the love of a certain person. You want
to determine the person who your main character desperately wants
to love and focus on that specific person. Your character doesn't want
just love, she wants the love of a specific man.

For example Romeo wants Juliet's love, Antony wants Cleopa-
tra's love. In *Titanic*, Rose desperately loves Jack and not her fiancé.
Now you can see how important it is to keep the goal from being abstract and to focus on the love of a specific person.

Another example of a goal that is not specific enough would be
a goal where your main character wants justice. Justice in itself is

too broad a goal and once again is too abstract. But if your main character wants to get justice against a big tobacco company which is addicting smokers and lying about it, then your character's goal is specific. It is imperative that you always give your main characters a specific goal to create momentum and conflict in your screenplay.

THE PROTAGONIST AND THE ANTAGONIST

The hero and the villain are known as the Protagonist (the hero) and the Antagonist (the villain). The protagonist has a goal that he desperately wants to reach and the opposing force that stands in his way is known as the antagonist. In action movies, this conflict is basically the good guys VS the bad guys. Audiences love this type of conflict because it gives them someone to root for and someone to fear.

If this is the type of conflict you want to write in your script, there are some important elements for you to know when using man against man conflict. You must develop clear contrast between your protagonist and antagonist. If you have someone to love, you need someone to hate or at least fear.

However, the protagonist must not be so strong that he overpowers his antagonist. Conversely, your hero must not be so weak that he'll not be a match for his antagonist. Each character must be of equal importance for you to have exciting and emotional conflict. If they are mismatched there is no conflict. One will win hands down, and who cares?

The stakes between your protagonist and antagonist must be high or your conflict will be weak. Therefore, the conflict must be of equal importance between the two characters. The fight between them must be an exciting contest. In either case, hero or opponent, the stakes must be high and the consequences of each not reaching his goal must be life-threatening.

When you watch any type of spectator sport, it is always better when the competition is equal. Certainly a tennis match between two top seated players is more exciting then a match between one of these talented men and a lower-ranked player. The more evenly matched the game the better the conflict and the harder the struggle. Well, the same is true for your protagonist and antagonist. The more evenly matched your hero and villain the more conflict and tension.

Just like human beings, your characters need to be multifaceted. They need at least one skeleton in their closet. If not a skeleton certainly they need to have a fault or two. You want to add layers to your characters as you write them. What internal conflicts do they have? What are the fears, phobias, hopes, dreams, and fantasies that create their inner life?

Characters should be well-balanced. Your opposition can't be all bad and your hero can't be all good. Be sure your hero has vulnerabilities. He must have a flaw or two so he'll be interesting. Perhaps he could possess a character trait he needs to overcome before he's able to reach his goal. Make him human by giving him a bad temper, or having him be fearful or insecure. Your antagonist certainly needs to have a few good qualities about him. He can't be all bad, can he? Maybe he volunteers as a Big Brother or at Meals on Wheels. Give your antagonist a many-sided personality which will intrigue the audience. Just like Hannibal Lecter in Thomas Harris' _Silence of the Lambs_. He is charming yet dangerous, smiling yet sinister, educated yet evil. What an exciting villain he is as well as an unforgettable one.

Do you recall Marlon Brando in _The Godfather_? Even though his character was responsible for the murder of many people, we see him at play with his grandson in his garden. We see his kindness towards his wife and children, and his concern for them as a husband and father.

When his son, Michael, who always refused to get involved in the family business, eventually becomes the Godfather, we understand his change because his actions are motivated. When members of another family try to kill his father and that's when Michael agrees to become the new Don.

This complex personality in Michael is strongly apparent during the Baptism scene in the Church. While he is behaving as a loving family man, a montage of scenes shows people being murdered. The irony is he's responsible for the murders occurring and being carried out against the backdrop of the church setting. This is character development at its best. We soon understand how and why he is such a contradiction.

THE "ESSED SYNDROME"

The more desperately your main character wants to reach his goal ~DEF,~
the more suspenseful and exciting your story. I always tell my students to make their characters have the ESSED syndrome: dis-
tressed, obsessed, suppressed, dispossessed, oppressed, stressed,
depressed, repressed, messed, or possessed. These are just a few adjectives that help describe the state of mind of a desperate, complex character. Your main character's desperation creates the
momentum that moves your story forward at an exciting, tension-
filled pace. You're not writing about the well-adjusted, happy
non-dysfunctional family, like *The Partridge Family* or the family in
Eight Is Enough.

Every character wants something in a script, and each character
is there to move the main character's story along to the climax. A
character shouldn't be in the story unless he or she helps move the
main character's story. The more desperately a character wants
something the more exciting your screenplay.

Great writing is about emotional conflict and we deal with stories
in which the characters have personal problems, thwarted dreams,
passionate goals. We aren't interested in stories that have no resolution to the conflict. We can experience that in real life, working in
dead-end jobs, being in never-ending relationships and living lives
of quiet desperation. ~WHY WE WATCH MOVIES~

When we view a film or television movie, we want to escape, to
see human beings who overcome the odds, who beat the system and
who conquer the forces of evil. This is what writing is all about. This
is why people pay for parking, baby sitters and movies so they can be
entertained and hopefully experience a catharsis along with the
main character's by the end of the film.

Characters don't just happen. It takes a lot of hard labor until you
give birth to well-rounded, three-dimensional characters. To help
you avoid some of the most prevalent flaws that writers make when
creating characters, I'm including the five most common ones and
techniques on how to avoid them. The following flaws are listed below to help you avoid making these mistakes before you begin to
develop your characters.

FIVE FATAL FLAWS FOR CREATING CHARACTERS

The five most fatal flaws which writers have for creating characters are:

1. All the characters sound the same.
2. The most boring and bland character is usually the main character—who is the writer in disguise.
3. The characters are based on real people, and the writer doesn't know how to make the characters dramatic.
4. The main character doesn't have a specific goal and is going nowhere.
5. "But that's the way it really happened" character syndrome.

TECHNIQUES TO AVOID THESE FIVE FATAL FLAWS

1. Putting parts of your inner selves into your characters to give them internal lives.
2. Capturing your emotional memories and giving these memories to your fictional characters.
3. Creating composite characters from people in your life, rather than creating a character based on just one person.
4. Setting goals that are specific and desperate for your characters so they have a destination and desperation.
5. Letting go of "how it really happened" and building characters who are based in reality, while fictionalizing them to be dramatic and memorable.

BLUEPRINT FOR SCREENWRITING

1. Who is the protagonist or main character?
2. What specific goal does the protagonist desperately want?
3. Who is the antagonist? Describe what the antagonist wants and why.
4. What are the high stakes the main character must suffer if he or she doesn't reach his or her goal?
5. Are the protagonist and antagonist of equal power and strength?
6. Does your main character have the ESSED syndrome and what is it?
7. What type of conflict does your main character face?
8. Do you have all three types of conflict in your screenplay? Describe.

Chapter 7
Creating the Character's Emotional Arc: The Heart of the Story

"When I used to teach creative writing, I would tell the students to make their characters want something right away."

—Kurt Vonnegut

The most important building block for your blueprint—to develop your characters with an emotional arc to prevent them from being flat and stereotypical. Your characters' internal world needs to have desires, regrets, hopes, dreams, fears, failures, love, resentments and many other emotions which reveal who they are under pressure and make your characters more emotionally complex.

Without an array of interesting and exciting characters your story just won't work and you must concentrate on how to develop characters with depth, with heart and with soul.

ANSWERING THE QUESTION "WHY?"

Many characters in scripts don't seem real because the writer forgets to address the most important question in writing: WHY?

The answer to "why" is the character's motivation as we discussed in the previous chapter. Motivation is what gives reality to your characters' quest or goal. Without knowing why characters behave as they do, a writer isn't able to make them real. So many writers just start writing without laying down the character's motivation. And they end up with are stock or stereotypical character's who aren't real or believable, because their behavior isn't motivated.

As a psychotherapist when I see new patients in my private practice I want to learn who they are in the present by understanding their past. I start by developing a case history for them to better understand their psychological profile, their drives, desires, and fears. To simplify I ask myself, "How did this individual get to be the person they are today?" "What happened to them in their childhood which still affects them now?" I look to their past for the answer. It's important for you to look to your characters' past history to understand why they behave they way they do, when you develop your story.

THE TIME LOCK (TICKING CLOCK) (DEAD LINES)

The more desperately your main character has to reach a specific goal the more exciting your story. Characters are revealed under stress or pressure. If your character isn't in a conflict or under pressure his real personality isn't revealed. You need to put your characters in a pressure cooker and watch how they act and react. One of the best ways of getting your main character under pressure is to use a "time lock." Put a time limit on the action your character takes and you'll have more suspense in your story.

If a character must discover a bomb that is about to go off in thirty minutes, you are putting a time lock on the situation. This is certainly more exciting than if the character had a week, or a month, to detonate the bomb. Put your main character into a situation with a time limit to reach her goal and you'll create the necessary pressure and tension to keep your audience interested.

The less time involved for your main character to reach his goal, the more compressed is the pressure and tension. Think of a kettle of water on the highest heat of a gas stove. You can't see inside the kettle to the exact moment the water turns to steam, but it surely will happen faster than when the kettle is on the lowest heat.

In another example, let's say your main character's goal is to get a job immediately, because she has to pay the rent. If she only has one week to find work, you'll create must more pressure on her than if she had a month. So a time limit is a wonderful devise to create more tension, conflict and suspense in your screenplay. In fact, the closer you set the opening of your screenplay to the ending or climax the more tension you have due to the shorter amount of time. It's always better to start your screenplay as close to the end as you possibly can.

Upping the Stakes

You can always make your main character's goal more desperate by "upping the stakes." Still using the above example if the character who needs a job is a lawyer or a doctor she probably won't have a difficult time finding one. But what if she is an unskilled worker? Chances are she would have to struggle to find work, since she has no marketable skills. This situation would certainly be more dramatic than if she were a highly qualified worker. Her lack of skills would cause her to have less chance to get a job.

We could up the stakes even more for this woman, especially if we make her not only an unskilled worker, but also a single mother with three children. If her children are hungry and she can't find work anywhere she is even more desperate. As the audience we are more involved in her plight. We care about her welfare and that of her children. Will she ever find a job? Will her children get sick from being hungry? Will she and her children become evicted from their apartment and end up homeless? What will she do in response to these pressures? Will she have to go on welfare? Will she shoplift to buy food for her children? Will they all become homeless?

These are called upping the stakes. By adding more and more pressure upon your character you increase the conflict. This kind of desperation makes your script fast-moving and exciting. Keep making the stakes higher and higher in order to increase the stress on your characters in your screenplay.

THE EXTERNAL (FALSE) AND INTERNAL (REAL) GOALS

The goal you choose for your main character in the opening of your screenplay is really the action or the story structure for your screenplay. Does the character want to be a prize fighter, play soccer, climb a mountain, overcome a disease? The main character's goal is what sets off your story in the opening of your screenplay as you can see from all of the above examples.

The goal gives your script movement, provides your protagoist with an objective to strive for throughout the story and furnishes your screenplay with a story. In all of the above illustrations we've only dealt with the character's external goal. This is often known as the false goal. A false goal is what the character thinks he wants, only to discover in the climax that it isn't.

However, there's another goal a character has in the script. This is known as the character's internal goal or real goal. All good screenplays and television movies include both the main character's external or false goal and internal or real goal. By having both types of goals you'll insure emotional depth to the entire script.

The following example will explain the difference between a false or external goal and a real or internal goal.

In _Tootsie_, a very well-structured classic screenplay, Dustin Hoffman's character, Michael Dorsey has a false goal, which is the storyline. The desperate goal is to get work as an actor. If his character was handsome and in demand like Brad Pitt that would be an easy and reachable goal. Then there'd be no conflict or script. But Michael Dorsey's goal is desperate, because he has such a difficult personality, that nobody will hire him. In desperation he disguises himself as a woman in order to get work on a television soap as a female lead.

Soon he has a successful role on the daytime show, and he eventually becomes the most popular character in the soap. In _Tootsie_ Michael has proven that he's able to act and he's reached his external goal. However, it's really his false goal. In the climax he discovers his real goal—wanting love of the Jessica Lange character. So in the end he even quits his successful acting job and reveals his love.

Having both the real and false goal gives depth to any script no matter what the genre. Let's take a detective story for example. In any detective story a crime is usually committed and must be solved. That is the basis for suspense and mystery.

If in the opening of the script a murder has taken place, the goal of the detective is to find out who committed the murder and to solve the crime. This sets-off the story and is the plot structure. It is the driving force of the script and gives our main character his action. However, it is really the detective's external or false goal.

Now, if solving a crime is all the story is about, it will have little depth. There are many mysteries which are written just like that. The only goal is for the detective to solve the crime. These types of scripts have been done thousands of times. They offer nothing fresh and original and are routine.

On the other hand, if in the process of solving the crime, Mr. Private Eye, the detective, learns something important about himself and experiences an emotional change or catharsis by the end of the script his character and the screenplay will be much deeper emotionally. This creates a more complex character and gives him greater depth, than if he only solved a crime. It also allows the audience to experience an emotional connection with the main character. They feel satisfied when in the end he discovers his own internal goal and experiences a psychological transformation.

Always try to include both the false goal and the real goal in your script. When you do you'll have a screenplay that is both powerful, emotional, fresh, and original!

THE EMOTIONAL LINE

The emotional line of your story is the emotional relationship between the main character and another major character. Although your main character interacts with many other characters, there is really only one other major character with whom he experiences the primary emotional relationship or connection.

In *Ordinary People*, the main character, Conrad, has relationships with many other characters—his mother, father, friends, coach, psychiatrist, girlfriend, friend from the hospital. However, his emotional line is between Conrad and his mother. Conrad desperately wants his mother's love and in the climax he discovers that she is incapable of loving him. His emotional change is that he finally realizes he will never get her love and that it's not his fault. He accepts that his mother doesn't love him as much as she loved his dead brother. That he has done nothing to cause this emotional pain, but his mother is just incapable of loving him in the way he wants her to.

This change was brought about by his struggle to get his mother's love throughout the story. Even though he doesn't receive her love, he is finally able to develop feelings of self-worth in spite of her. In the climax, Conrad comes to a new level of understanding about his mother. For the first time he accepts her as she is. But his main change is his ability to like himself regardless of how she treats him. Conrad has experienced an emotional transformation or change and he's different from who he was in the beginning of the story. To put it in simple terms he has gone from being insecure to being secure. Remember what I said earlier, that the main character must experience a change! In the climax of *Ordinary People*, Conrad changed, as Michael did in *Tootsie*. In both examples each character experienced an emotional change and an emotional transformational arc.

In every screenplay there needs to be a character arc so that we see the character change from one emotional state to another, thereby revealing the character's emotional growth.

One of the biggest criticisms of movie, *A.I.* is you didn't care about anyone in the film, which was proliferated with so many special effects that the emotional line was lost. You weren't even involved with the main character, which was quite a contrast to *E.T.* Both films about aliens were made by Steven Spielberg. In *A.I.* there was no strong emotional line between any of the characters, while in *E.T.* there were powerful emotional relationships between *E.T.* and his human friends, who loved him and wanted to help him go home.

Even in action adventure films, when there is strong action plus a powerful emotional relationship between the main character and another major character, you have greater depth, you have fireworks, you have drama! Some of the successful adventure films which also include an emotional relationship are such classics as:

Expls.

The African Queen, Raiders of the Lost Ark, and the recent film, *The Gladiator*. These worked because they included both levels—plot and emotional line—making us care about the characters throughout all their adventures. We hope they will survive the danger together. By the end of these adventures we root for these characters to be safe.

THE CHARACTER'S EMOTIONAL TRANSFORMATION

Expl.

Continuing to use *Tootsie* as an example, Michael Dorsey who didn't care about anything else but acting in the beginning, now discovers he needs love. In fact, in the beginning of the film he treated women more as objects than as equals. He really never wanted to be get romantically involved or fall in love with anyone. Yet, by the end of the picture he realizes what's important to him and experiences an emotional transformation. He has learned how to be a better man through being a woman and recognizing how badly he'd treated women in his past relationships.

ARC

As you create your main character ask yourself what her transformational arc will be in the climax. What emotional change will she experience from the opening through to the ending. Obviously, she will have to make personal changes throughout your story, little by little, and not all at once. When a baby learns to walk he first starts to crawl and then step by step eventually learns how to walk. Falling down a lot and getting hurt in the process is part of his growth. Well, the same is true for your main character's personal growth.

When your main character experiences a change or transformation in the climax, it will be believable and not forced if you have motivated the change throughout your entire script in every scene. If a character becomes courageous in the climax, he would have to be fearful in the beginning of your story. That's his emotional transformation. He must develop and struggle throughout the script in order to emotionally change from fearful to brave.

In fact, if a character doesn't change in the climax your screenplay still could work only if you make your character struggle and remain active throughout the script. That's how William Shakespeare's tragedies worked, because Othello, King Lear and

Expl,

In a tragedy, the protagonist struggles with his weakness, and in the end, looses to it.

Macbeth all struggled throughout, but in the end their fatal flaw caused their individual downfall.

It will be helpful if you can describe your character's emotional transformational arc by using an adjective or verb as follows: "My main character goes from hate to love; from selfish to selfless; from weak to strong." This will help you determine the emotional line of your main character and determine what their emotional transformation will be in the climax.

How people act, respond, react, and most important— FEEL—is what makes good drama. It is how characters behave with one another and how they react and interact in friendship or love that makes for strong emotional writing. It is the emotional story people pay to see. They want to be moved, to feel and to care. By concentrating on the character's emotional transformation of your story you will be laying down complex characters who experience a transformational arc and will make your screenplay successful and riveting.

EMOTION LINE

BLUEPRINT FOR SCREENWRITING

1. What is your main character's external or false goal?
2. Does your character's behavior seem believable and consistent with his personality? Explain.
3. Write a scene where you are "upping the stakes" for your story.
4. What is your main character's internal motivation or real goal?
5. What is your main character's emotional transformation? Describe.
6. Create a time lock for your screenplay? Describe how it increases the tension.

→ Describe your protagonist's arc
from pole to pole as: from:
fear to courage, isolation to family,
hate to love, etc., p.65

Chapter 8

The Psychology of Characters

"Writing is a form of therapy."

—Graham Greene

Just as you can't "Judge a book by its cover," you can't judge a person by the way he looks or behaves. You probably know from your own experience that the way you portray yourself to others may be entirely different from the way you are feeling inside. Perhaps you feel insecure when you first meet people, but do you tell them how frightened you're feeling inside? No. You smile, try to be pleasant and make conversation. Little do they know your palms are sweaty and you have butterflies flying around inside your stomach. You are acting one way and feeling another and trying to get those butterflies to fly in formation.

Well, you're not alone! Most everyone feels exactly as you do! All of us live inside ourselves. We all wear masks and only on those rare moments are we able to connect to another person in a meaningful way. This accounts for the feelings of isolation and alienation among people in our society today. We have a complete internal life apart from other people and known only to us alone. And if we're lucky there may be a handful of friends or family who get glimpses of who we really are.

When you begin to create your characters you must not only think about their emotional, social, and physical aspects, but also their internal life. Ask yourself if your character is behaving like an extrovert, but is really feeling shy inside? Do you have a beautiful female character who feels ugly inside? Is your character a mild-mannered young man, just waiting to explode?

Think of all your characters as you would think of your fellow human beings. Give them the same internal problems humans have, so they will come alive and be real. You need to develop the psychology of your characters to avoid the stereotypical or stock characters you see in B movies.

Imagine some of the conflicts you have in your every day life— feelings of self-doubt, insecurity, lust, hate, love, pain, loneliness, depression and rage. To be alive is to feel! Feelings are the true barometer of who you really are. What are your character's hopes? What does he fear? What is he struggling for? What does he desperately want? How does he feel inside about himself? Is he confident, insecure, doubtful, narcissistic, secure, afraid, angry, egotistical? Can you find the right adjectives to best describe your character?

MAKE A LIST USING A THESAURUS TO DESCRIBE CHARACTER TRAITS

Look in a thesaurus and make a list of all the adjectives you can think of for your character's personality. What one adjective best suits his over-all personality? Which adjective describes your characters most prominent personality trait. Write it down and when you put your character in situations, think of the adjective that best describes him. This will give you a handle to capture the essence of your character and find his core. Do this for all of your characters and you will see how consistent and realistic they will become.

Expls.

Think of some of the all time classics that never stop being popular even though they were made years ago. Some of these films are *Casablanca, Gone With the Wind, Dirty Harry, All About Eve, To Kill a Mockingbird* to name a few. What are your favorite classics? And why?

It's the characters who make these film memorable, because they're able to withstand the test of time. These characters are so well-developed and layered that you probably were able to immediately think of the most accurate description for each one. What are the characteristics that make Scarlett and Rhett; Ilsa and Rick; Eve and Margo; Atticus Finch and Harry so larger than life and layer human beings. It's their psychology that plays a major part in making them outstanding.

Try to describe the various character traits of each of the above characters. List them on a piece of paper and next to each name write down the best adjective or adverb for each one. By doing this you'll discover that each major role can be described by a major characteristic, which creates the character's motivation, conflict and dialogue.

Who are some of the major characters you remember and like in other classic films? Do you understand what characteristic makes each character unique? Using this method of relating a major characteristic with your own characters will enable you to create ones who will be memorable and outstanding. *CHARACTER DRIVEN PERSONAL FILMS*

Let's face it, there are no new plots under the sun. There are only character's who make a film stand out from all the rest. Just look at the success of the small personal films that are more character driven and contain little if any plot. It's because the characters are fresh and aren't the same tired, cliched ones that you see in most films. Some of these films are American Splendor, The Whale Rider, and Pieces of April. These are quiet films yet they're filled with emotional conflict because of the main character interacting in relationship to other characters. *Expla,* *MAKE CHARACTERS COMPLEX AND MULTI DIMENSIONAL*

The successful characters in classic films display additional personality traits beside the major one. This is why they are complex characters, rather than one dimensional, multifaceted rather than stereotypical. By developing a major characteristic for your characters, plus knowing their quirks, neurosis and flaws, you will create three dimensional characters with many personality traits, yet still have a basic spine or core personality. *WHY DOES HE FEEL THAT WAY?*

After you have thought about all of his internal feelings, you need to find out why your character feels as he does. To discover the answer to "why" means you must go deeply into your character's past, asking all kinds of pertinent questions along the way. Just as a psychologist asks questions of his patient to get a case history, you must ask questions of your character to get his past history.

15 × p L.   Who raised him? Did she have a happy childhood? Where did
she grow up? Were his parents divorced or were they happily married? Did he have any brothers or sisters or was he the only child?
Was she the oldest child or the youngest? In school did he have a lot
of friends? Was she a loner? Was he popular and did he belong to the
"in" crowd or was he the class "nerd?" Did she date or didn't she like
boys? Did he get good grades or was he a poor student? How did she
get along with her parents, siblings, friends, relatives?

Keep asking these types of in-depth questions to get a vivid past
life of your character, up until the time you first introduce him in
your story. Your character does not live in a vacuum, and he must
have a past history that you develop. To learn his history you must
play psychologist. You need to discover why he acts as he does in the
present by studying his past.

By the time you finish creating a personal life for each character,
you will know his parents, his grandparents and even his great-
grandparents. By developing a history for your character, you will be
able to understand his present behavior and be able to develop the
necessary motivations for his present actions.

PSYCHOLOGY OF A CHARACTER: A CASE STUDY

As a writer, behaving like a psychologist, you are always probing
more deeply inside your character's skin, always questioning his behavior. You are searching for reasons for his actions and creating
motivation for them. Let's suppose your character is hungry. Being
hungry will motivate him to find food to eat.

Hunger is the stimulus and finding food is his response to hunger.
This is easy enough to understand. He might simply open the refrigerator or freezer and grab something to eat. If they are both empty
he could go to a restaurant or store and buy some food. These are
easy solutions to the problem of being hungry. But what if he doesn't
have any food in his home? What if he doesn't have a home? What if
he doesn't have any money to purchase food? What will he do?

Now you must consider not only a character's motivation (hunger), you must also consider his internal make-up. If he is amoral or
asocial he might rob a bank, break into a house or mug a person to

get money for food. If he is moralistic and doesn't believe in breaking the law, he might ask his friends to lend him some money for food. If he is resourceful, he might go fishing or hunting and use his environment to find food. If he is conniving or he manipulates others, he might devise a scheme to bring him a quick buck for food.

His value system, his beliefs, his past experiences, his abilities, and his personality will determine his behavior when he is faced with a specific stimulus like hunger. Yet, there is another aspect to his motivation. It is the degree of hunger that will determine to what lengths he will go to obtain food. With this in mind, don't ever say, "My character would never steal," or "My character would never have an affair."

Given the right set of circumstances, enough desperation, and a hostile environment, you can motivate your character to steal, in a way that would be believable. It's amazing what human beings are capable of doing under the right circumstances, especially in life and death situations. If you give your characters the proper motivation and the right situation, anything is possible for them to do, especially if they are desperate.

Thus, The way your character satisfies his needs depends on what choices and circumstances are available to him at a given time. What if he is hungry and happens to be in prison or in the armed forces? In each case he is at the mercy of other people and his behavior is restricted by his superiors and their rules and regulations. Obviously, he is unable to make the choices he would like to make, because there would be harmful consequences to his actions.

Remember not only to deal with your character's need, but also with how he behaves in getting his need met. This depends on the desperation of the need, the environment and his value and belief system. The most important determination for his behavior will be the many characteristics and traits that make up his personality. The more complex your character, the more varied his personality traits. These internal character traits will create conflicts within your character and keep him from being a stock character.

After you have developed the past history for your character and his complete character biography, you will want to study the relationship between his outer self and his internal self.

"What is the relationship between your character's physical appearance and his emotional state?"

"Where does he live and how does his environment affect his self-esteem?"

Start looking for cause-and-effect connections between all aspects of your character's life. Look for connections between your character's inner life and outer world. Is your character playing a role or is he being authentic?

Another type of frustration your character can encounter is outside of himself. The frustration could be environmental and could include: lack of money, sickness, lack of employment, or lack of friends, just to name a few. These types of frustrations are the external obstacles that create conflict for your character. They are the stumbling blocks that stand in the way of him reaching his goal. He must overcome them to succeed.

How your character deals with his internal and external frustrations will depend on the psychology of your character. Sometimes reducing a frustration can be easy. If your character is always late, he can make an effort to be on time, especially if he is threatened with losing his job for tardiness. If he is unable to pay his bills because he spends too much money he can start a budget and economize. He reduces his frustration and overcomes the obstacle.

Yet, there are some cases where the conflict persists even though he desperately wants to solve it. Suppose he is a drug addict or an alcoholic. He is threatened with losing his wife and his job, unless he quits his addiction. He may desperately want to quit drugs or alcohol and he may suffer from terrible feelings of guilt and self-disgust when he can't quit.

He is not in control and may ask himself, "Why can't I stop this destructive habit?"

He swears over and over he'll never do it again … and yet … he can't stop. Your character is suffering from an internal conflict that he can't resolve even though he desperately wants to. He might continue this behavior until something from his environment motivates him to change. Perhaps his wife and children leave him or his buddy dies from an overdose. These circumstances might be strong enough to motivate him into his giving up his addiction.

On the other hand, he might fall to the bottom of the barrel and end up on skid row, a beaten, defeated addict. How he will act or react will be determined by the psychological make-up that you have created for his character. Your audience will understand and believe in your character, as he reveals himself under pressure, only if you have done a good job in making his actions believable and consistent with his personality.

Your audience will root for your character and sympathize with his plight, even in cases where he doesn't succeed, as long as your character struggles. It is the struggle that is of prime importance when dealing with obstacles he must overcome that stand in the way of his goal.

Read books on abnormal psychology. Observe people around you, at work, home, and play. Put yourself inside your character's head and get to understand what he thinks and feels. Peel the layers of protective covering away as you put your character under pressure. Strip your character of his defenses and watch what he does.

Presently, the motion picture industries are dealing with sensitive issues such as child abuse, wife abuse, suicide, sexual abuse, addiction, divorce, homosexuality, personality disorders, and many mental health issues. I am often called in as a consultant to work with writers, producers and directors, on specific psychological aspects of their scripts and their characters, to make certain they are treated accurately and realistic.

For you as a screenwriter it is not enough just to deal with these issues. You must know the effects of different abuses on the victim and her family. What happens to the wife and children of an alcoholic? What are the long term effects of sexual molestation? How does a child behave who is a victim of child abuse? What happens to the survivors of a suicide victim? How are adult children of alcoholics affected by their parents drinking? What are the characteristics of a co-dependent couple? How do people cope after divorce?

All of these issues must be dealt with honestly and openly. That is why people in the industry consult with professionals in the mental health field, so when these issues are the subject of the film, the characters will behave in a realistic way.

A year ago, I worked with a woman who was writing a screenplay about adoption. After she completed her script she came to see me,

Read about disfunctional psychology and deviant behavior.

because she wasn't satisfied with her script. I was amazed at how inaccurate her portrayal of her leading character, a young woman who recently discovered she was adopted. The writer hadn't put any emotion into the main character, in fact, the young woman wasn't emotionally confused or torn about discovering that the parents she'd loved and known weren't her birth parents.

The writer wasn't able to give her main character emotions because she not only hadn't done research on the psychological effects of adoption, but also had no idea what happens to an adopted child on an emotional level. Her main characters emotional behavior was so unrealistic that her entire script didn't work.

Before I worked with her on character development, I first worked with her on her own emotions, taking her back to the time, when she discovered a family secret and how she'd felt when she realized the truth. I had her do some free writing about the experience and her feelings of shock and betrayal.

She eventually was able to get in touch with those painful memories and then was freed up emotionally to put her real feelings into her female character. Suddenly, she was behaving in a realistic and credible manner, because the screenwriter was able to put the truth of her own emotions into her character. She added layers to her and made her script very powerful and emotionally truthful.

With today's worldly and sophisticated audiences, you must have knowledge of such psychological issues as death, divorce, rape, incest, alcoholism, abuse and dysfunctional relationships to name a few. These and other mental health issues are frequently written about in today's scripts, especially the real life stories on television, which usually have to do with murder, mayhem, death, divorce and dysfunction. You have to get in touch with your own psychological issues, so you'll be able to put them into your characters, just so the characters will be portrayed in an accurate and realistic way.

You must do your research if you write about serious topics that have deep psychological effects on the victim and other members of the family. You must know what happens to people when they experience disturbing or deviant behavior, and realistically show the ramifications of these experiences on your characters.

Most good writers are good psychologists. Think of Shakespeare, Ibsen, Chekov, Tolstoy, to name a few. These writers understood the human condition. They were psychologists probing the inner depths of their characters and dealing with their frailties, fears, and frustrations. Each one of these writers had a wonderful knowledge of human nature. They created memorable characters who have withstood the test of time.

There is much more to writing a story then creating a plot and characters. When you begin to understand the psychology of your characters, you will be on the road to building complex, interesting characters who will be remembered long after your work is completed.

BLUEPRINT FOR SCREENWRITING

1. What are the internal frustrations of your main character?
2. How do these frustrations affect the character's relationships?
3. Does your main character have any addictions or secrets? Write about them in-depth.
4. Write an intensive past history of your main character's psychology?
5. Describe your main character's relationship with family and friends.
6. What is your main character's psychological make-up? Describe in detail.
7. List some of your main character internal conflicts.
8. How does she manifest these conflicts?
9. List the many character traits of your major characters. Find the one to best describe each character and why this trait fits your character.
10. What is the relationship between your character's physical appearance and his emotional state? P. 72
11. Where does he live and how does his environment affect his self esteem? p 72
12 what is the deviant behavior and disfunctional psychology of your characters? Research them to make your characters real,

Chapter 9

Structuring Scenes and Acts

"If I didn't know the ending of a story I wouldn't begin. I always write my last line, my last paragraphs, my last page first."

—Katherine Ann Porter

Screenwriting is a craft onto itself, having a special format, specific margins, a definite number of pages, and a highly developed structure. Starting a new screenplay is often like beginning a new relationship. When you first meet the love of your life, aren't you enthusiastic and excited, putting all your energy into it? After months or years of dating or getting married, doesn't your enthusiasm wane because of all the effort, energy and hard work it takes to keep your relationship viable and alive? Well, it's the same with writing scenes.

By now your blueprint for screenwriting is almost completed. You've laid down the foundation, constructed the framework, built your story and developed your characters. Now, you need to design your blueprint into a definite structure.

SCREENWRITING—ACT AND SCENES

Anything worth doing well takes hard work and unfortunately, so many people don't appreciate or respect the craft of screenwriting and how difficult it actually is. Ideas are a dime a dozen, but it's the actual execution of the ideas put into 108–120 pages of script that takes self-discipline, hard work and commitment. Writers often think of new ideas when they're stuck in Act 2 or they have problems with the Act 3 climax. Other writers get discouraged when they're beginning at Fade In and realize they have over 100 more pages to go. They usually wonder what to do, because everything seems so unwieldy and they have no idea. The thought of having over 100 pages of script from beginning to end can seem quite formidable to anyone.

To make writing a screenplay more manageable you need to break down your 108–120 pages into scenes and acts. This allows your material to be easier to write and you won't lose your way in the middle of your script.

Today, with the popularity of novels being made into films, many novelists would like to adapt their own fiction into a screenplay if only they knew how. That is why so many novels that are adapted into screenplays aren't written by the novelist, but by a screenwriter. The two forms of writing are so completely different. Screenwriting has specific rules and the construction has to deal with your structure. Story structure is what good screenwriting is all about—a blueprint for laying out a story.

By now your blueprint for screenwriting is almost completed. You've laid down the foundation, constructed the framework, built your story and developed your characters. Now, you need to design your blueprint into a definite structure.

When you build a home it must have a floor plan showing the number of floors and the layout of the rooms on each floor. When you construct your screenplay it must have a layout, which is made up of scenes and acts.

The average length of a motion picture or a television movie is approximately 90 minutes to two hours. Knowing this approximate time limit is helpful, because it allows you to write the correct number of pages for your screenplay, since each page of screenplay equals a minute of film. A screenplay with 120 pages would be a two hour film.

A sure sign that you're a beginner would be if you'd write a 300 page screenplay. Nobody would read it let alone buy it. They will have neither the time nor the inclination. It will be clear to them that you don't understand the craft of screenwriting, which consists of acts and scenes written in a specific amount of pages.

The Purpose of a Scene

What is a scene? A scene is a unit of drama, just as a brick is a unit of a building. You lay out each scene as you would lay bricks on a building. Each scene is laid down upon the scene preceding it, just as each brick is laid upon another brick. By constructing your scenes this way you will build a solid foundation for all the scenes in your screenplay. Every scene you write must be connected, from your opening scene, which sets up the problem, through to the climactic scene which ends your screenplay.

A scene, like your screenplay, has a beginning, a middle, and an end. You can think of your scene as a mini-screenplay, having all the same elements. In other words, your scene starts at one point of action and leads to another, which is the climax or end of your scene. As in a screenplay, you need to know the ending of your scene first, before you start writing it, and work backwards from your ending to the opening.

Every scene has a purpose. Without a purpose, the scene doesn't work. Before any students in my class write a scene, I have them ask, "What is the purpose or overall reason of this scene?"

Finding the purpose of your scene helps to give your scene focus. Perhaps the purpose of your scene is to introduce a love interest, show a crime being committed, or to plant a necessary clue for a detective to discover. Knowing your purpose keeps your writing solid and on track, and gives you a direction to follow. Can you tell your scene in a sentence or two?

START THE SCENE IN

The Middle of the Action

If you're writing a scene that shows a man taking a woman on a first date, where is the best place to start the scene? The best place to start your scene is in the middle of the action! The middle of the action means exactly what it says. The couple on a first date could be sitting together in a restaurant having dinner. Or they could be driving in his car on the way to a party.

You would never start your scene showing him driving to her apartment, parking the car, walking down the street to the apartment entrance, ringing the bell to enter, waiting for the elevator, riding the elevator to her floor, knocking at her door and introducing himself to her when she opens the door. This is all unnecessary and boring. Who cares how he gets to her apartment? It would slow down your story and waste time because nothing is happening!

On the other hand, if you want to show something happen to the man on the way to her apartment, then you would need to start the scene with him going to it. Maybe on the way to her apartment the man gets mugged or he sees a robbery in progress. Then it would be necessary to open the scene showing him on his way to pick her up, if that is the purpose of your scene. It is important for you to know what you want to accomplish in the scene before you start writing. If you can't state the purpose in a sentence or two, then rethink your scene or eliminate it, because it isn't focused.

Scene Connections and Progression

When you start a scene it must go somewhere. By the end of the scene the character is at a higher point of drama then before. All scenes must have a climax or ending, that leads the character to the next scene, otherwise your writing is episodic and without a direction or a structure.

Now you know that all scenes have a beginning, a middle and an end, and they also must have a definite direction. A scene can be as short as half a page or as long as five or more pages. Whatever the length, the elements you should include are: (a) have a beginning, a middle, a climax; (b) start in the middle of the action; (c) have conflict; (d) have a single purpose to the scene.

Since film is visual, all scenes must have movement throughout the screenplay. In the climax of a scene something must happen, just as it happens in the climax of a screenplay. The climax of your scene must be the most dramatic point and further the action along to the next scene. A scene should thrust your story forward, compelling the audience to ask, "What's going to happen next?"

Every new scene must germinate from the previous scene and lead to the scene that follows. There must be a connection between every scene so as to avoid episodic writing. Besides making your scenes connect they must lead toward the climax of your screenplay. Every scene needs to move the story to the end, making your screenplay an exciting journey.

Dramatic Conflict in Scenes

All scenes must have DRAMATIC CONFLICT! Without dramatic conflict you have nothing but either exposition or flat conversation. Since the audience is interested in emotional relationships, your conflict should create emotional conflict between characters. Conflict doesn't have to consist of battles, fights or wars. It's the emotional conflict that can have more dramatic impact in a scene than all the explosions and special effects in the world.

Dramatic conflict can involve the main character wanting something and someone standing in the way of him getting what he wants. This adds dramatic tension and suspense to all your scenes. A man driving a car down the street isn't conflict. But a man driving a car with someone holding a gun to his head is dramatic conflict. Without conflict there is no drama. *HOW to DO IT.*

For every scene you write ask yourself: "What is the dramatic conflict in this scene?" *The extreme emotional conflict* *PLUS comic RELIEF p. 83*

"What does my main character want in this scene and who is preventing her from getting it?"

If you can't find the answers, don't write the scene. There are *Chase Scenes* scenes that are known as a sequence of scenes. They may be described as chase scenes, where there can be many different locations, but where there is still only one purpose. A great example of a sequence of scenes is the chase scene in *Basic Instinct*. The purpose of the scenes was for Michael Douglas, playing a detective, to catch the person who just murdered his partner and is now speeding away. The locations throughout San Francisco were varied and there were near misses along the chase, but there still was only one *Expl.*

The chase scene was when the lesbian lover tried to kill Michael's character. The partner died in an elevator (ice picks) w/no chase scene, as I recall.

purpose—to catch the person, driving the car, who he suspected of murdering his partner.

WRITING CAUSAL SCENES

Between the opening scene that sets off your story and the climactic scene that ends your story, you may have as many as 50 to 80 scenes. Each of the scenes must connect to the other in a cause-and-effect manner. Although each scene must stand alone, as a complete unit of drama, it must also evolve from the scene that preceded it and lead to the scene that follows it.

Screenwriting is known as causal writing, because one scene causes the next scene and so until the end. All the scenes in a screenplay build upon one another to develop the plot structure. If you remove one of the scenes your entire story structure should collapse. When people write episodic scenes they can be removed and nothing changes the overall plot because they weren't connected in the first place. That's why they're considered episodic.

You can compare removing scenes from a screenplay to removing beams from a building. Both would topple over if you removed an integral part from the structure. If removing a scene doesn't affect your overall screenplay then the scene is not necessary and should be eliminated. Think of your scenes as your would a house. Without the steel frames or skeleton, your house would topple over just like your screenplay.

However, if you remove a scene in a cohesive screenplay your entire structure should collapse and your screenplay fail. If a scene doesn't relate to your overall plot structure, don't use the scene, even if it's a terrific one.

How do you determine which scenes to include in your script? You do this by first deciding if it relates to your storyline. So you need to be able to state your storyline in a couple of sentences in order to know if the scene relates to the overall plot. Ask yourself if the scene helps move your story forward and if it doesn't, remove the scene, because it doesn't belong in your screenplay.

You have to choose what scenes you need to write for your screenplay to fulfill your structure. The first thing to do is start thinking of all the possible scenes you want in your screenplay. Let your imagination really go wild. Then jot down every scene you could conceivably use in your screenplay. Let your mind expand and free associate your ideas. Write everything that comes into your head in a couple sentences for each potential scene. It doesn't matter if you discard most of them, it's important to get them down without judgment.

Next, imagine all the situations that could possibly happen to your main character in order for him to reach his goal. Put down everything that comes into your mind. Think of your settings, of the characters, of the locations, atmosphere, the obstacles and write them down as fast as you can. After you have written all of the possibilities you can imagine, then start concerning yourself with putting the scenes in some order.

It is always a good idea to pace your scenes. Follow a strong emotional scene with a quiet scene. An action scene should be preceded by a slower-paced scene. Quiet scenes can be very powerful. They can include moments of introspection, when a character discovers something about himself or another character.

Remember the value of comic relief. When things get too emotionally heavy use your humor to give your audience relief from the intensity. Watch films that succeed in pacing the scenes and develop your sensitivity as a writer to pace your scenes throughout and intersperse humor with drama.

[handwritten margin notes: PACING / 1. QUIET SCENE / 2. COMIC RELIEF SCENE]

THE THREE-ACT STRUCTURE

To structure your scenes in the correct order you need to know the three act format and what elements must go into each act. Breaking your screenplay into acts will allow you to have a blueprint to follow. This permits writing the screenplay to be more manageable and broken down into sections. It is much more easy to construct than it would be by trying to write 120 pages straight through. Breaking your screenplay into a three act structure gives you a guide to follow on your writing journey.

Act I—The Exposition *(handwritten: The CHALLENGE & SET-UP)*

Act I is known as the act of Exposition. It is approximately 30 pages in length (1–30). In the opening of Act I you must set-up the problem to be solved and the dramatic question that needs to be answered. In Act I you also introduce the main and major characters of your film. This problem will take the rest of the movie to solve. The audience must immediately know what your movie is about or they will lose interest. They should understand what's going on and care about the problem confronting the main character. I always tell my students to ask themselves when they open their screenplay: "Why is this day in the life of my character different from any other day in his life?"

Something must happen to start your story moving toward a destination. What event or problem starts your main character on a journey? Is it a death, divorce, losing a job or meeting the person of your dreams? You need to know what your story is about and your viewers want to know what world you're taking them to visit, what are the rules and who are the players. There is nothing worse than reading a book or seeing a movie and not knowing what's happening.

We live in an age of "I want it now," with fast food deliveries, instant microwave dinners, and drive through restaurants. Just push a button and you can buy anything you want on the Home Shopping Channel, get money from the ATM machine and instantly interact with video and computer games. So it's understandable that more screenwriters try to hook the viewers in the first three minutes, and less than ten minutes. Longer than this period of time will make your viewer bored and perhaps ask for his money back from the theater.

If your audience isn't hooked immediately you have failed your goal as a screenwriter. A good way to check to see if you have all the necessary elements in Act I is to ask: "What does my main character desperately want?" (His goal.) "What is the problem I'm introducing for my main character to solve?" "Am I starting my screenplay with an immediate problem?" "Do I hook and interest my audience by the first ten pages?"

When you can answer "yes" to these questions, you then have the right elements for Act I. By the end of Act I, all the information should be given to your audience, and they should know what dramatic question needs to be solved. They also should have all the background and information they need to understand your story. By the end of Act I your main character is taking action and moving forward. There is no turning back. He has made a decision to solve the problem and is moving ahead.

Act II—The Complications (THE BATTLE)

Act II is known as the Act of Complications. Act II is the longest act. It consists of approximately 60 pages (30–90). In Act II you must set up all of the obstacles that stand in the path of your main character. The more stumbling blocks you put in his path to prevent him from reaching his goal, the more your main character must struggle to reach it. In Act II the conflict and tension must escalate to a higher point than in Act I.

ALL IS LOST

By the end of Act II it looks as if "all is lost" for your main character. The audience is on the edge of their seats not knowing what will happen to the hero. Your main character is at his lowest and most desperate point. It looks as if he is has nowhere to go.

In the last scene of Act II he is at the point of no return and must take some new and dramatic action. He is forced to make a new decision that leads him to do something different. He is really at the crossroads or turning point. This act is probably the most difficult for people to write, because you need to keep the conflict moving and increasing with intensity.

It seems when writers get stuck it's usually in the middle of the second act. You need to have every scene build-up in conflict and complications and lead into the next building greater suspense and tension. This involves the best of craft and takes a lot of practice, so that your second act doesn't fall apart in the middle.

Act III—The Resolution

Act III is known as the act of Resolution. It is the shortest act in the screenplay. It has approximately 30 pages or even less (90–120). All that has gone on before is heading to the highest point of dramatic conflict—the climax. The climax is the end of your screenplay. In Act III the problems you set-up in the opening must be resolved; your main character must experience a change; and your theme must be revealed. In Act III your main character makes a discovery about himself. He "sees the light" so to speak, and learns something

INSIGHT

about himself he didn't know throughout your screenplay. As he gains new insight about himself, your audience will feel satisfied.

All of the preceding scenes of your screenplay have been leading up to this climactic one. If the action escalates in the second act, by Act III the action explodes in the climax. When the climax is over, your story is over. Nothing else can happen. If you continue your screenplay after the climax, it will be considered anti-climactic. You'll be left with a weak ending and a dissatisfied audience. So be sure to end your screenplay when the climax ends.

The Denouement (A TAG)

However, after the climax there is a final quick scene which is known as a tag. It is referred to as the denouement. In the film, *Cold Mountain*, the denouement is not when Jude Law and Nicole Kidman, who played the romantic leads, apart for four years, finally get together, make love. This is the climax. The denouement is seeing a child years later which is their love child. It's the scene following the climax.

The denouement is like tying the story up in a neat package with a bright red ribbon. It is the "and then they lived happily ever after." In a detective story the denouement is after the mystery has been solved and you see the detectives having a drink together happy about solving the case.

By breaking your screenplay down into three acts it will help you develop your scenes in the right structure. It allows you to deal with a smaller unit of work and gives you a Blueprint for Screenwriting for each act.

BLUEPRINT FOR SCREENWRITING

1. Do you immediately grab your audience by the first 3–10 pages? How?
2. In Act I what dramatic problem or question do you set up for your main character to solve?
3. Write in a sentence or two the purpose of each scene you've written.
4. Write a scene after the climax—your denouement.
5. Create complications and obstacles to put in the path of your main character's goal in Act II.
6. In Act III is your climax at the end of your story or is it anti-climactic? Is the theme revealed?
7. Do all your previous scenes lead to the climax?
8. Does you main character solve the problem in the climax? How?

Chapter 10

The Outline,
The Treatment,
The Synopsis

"I usually make detailed outlines: How many chapters it will be and so forth."
—John Barth

When you want to get started on a new project, try to first write your story in prose, just as you would a short story. You need to get your thoughts down and not worry about script format, until you have some knowledge of the story you want to write for your script.

THE SYNOPSIS *(1-5 pages)*

Summary of story written in prose, telling

These pages of prose, when perfected, will be known as your synopsis for your screenplay. A synopsis should be not less than one page and not more than five pages. It should tell your complete story in prose from beginning to end. Many times a production company, studio or network will only ask for a synopsis before they decide if they want to read your entire script.

You can see why your synopsis must be an exciting piece of prose. You want to give the broader story in a synopsis, rather than a detailed description of everything that happens. This would make your synopsis too unwieldy and too long. You want to use broad brush strokes when you write your synopsis, revealing just enough to titillate your reader. A well-written synopsis is important in that it can create interest in your script.

Writing a synopsis helps you get your story down as best as you can before you begin your outline. It is written as you would write a short story, in present tense prose, and helps give you an overview of your script. It is less structured then an outline and often accompanies a feature length script or teleplay. This occurs when the producer, director or publisher don't want to read your entire script or manuscript and ask you write up a synopsis. Sometimes this is very difficult, especially after you've completed your script, because they might only want to read a one page synopsis.

Here is an example of a synopsis of a recent screenplay that I wrote with Brenda Krantz my collaborator. "Stingers" is a horror script and this is our synopsis.

"STINGERS"
SYNOPSIS

by
Brenda Krantz and Rachel Ballon

JOSH FIELDING, in his late teens is a lab assistant to MAX GARRING, an Entomologist at the local university. He is going home for the summer to Bellefonte in order to help his father, a bee keeper, with the hives. Max is a hero to the local farmers, because he has developed a milder killer bee to replace the aggressive ones which had been over-powering the honeybees who pollinate the crops. Now the farmers will have abundant crops once more all because of Max.

Josh goes home to his beautiful girlfriend, Kirstin and his coterie of friends—Derek, Ben, Alicia—where they plan to party and hang out during the summer vacation. No sooner does Josh arrive home when he and Ben almost hit a dog lying mutilated in the road. There are Stingers protruding from his body. After that hideous discovery things go from bad to worse and strange deaths occur in a grotesque and sickening manner. Ben's sister and her baby are found with dead with STINGERS swaying throughout their distorted bodies.

Max soon realizes he has to destroy all the bees he has sent to the farmers and to his sister FRIEDA GARRING, who is the proprietor of FRIEDA's BEE CLINIC. There she runs a thriving business administering bee sting therapy, and selling Pheromone and Royal Jelly to her loyal clientele. Frieda will do everything in her power to prevent her brother from destroying her bees. Besides, their relationship is contentious and filled with sibling jealousy. She'd like nothing better than to see her brother be humiliated and fail.

Josh calls Max and accuses him of creating some type of monster—a mutant "Botbee" who lays larvae inside humans and beasts, by entering through their mucus membrane orifices and taking over their bodies as incubating hives. Max denies any wrong doing and refuses to help stem the rising danger. It is now up to Josh, with the help of his friends, to prevent these aggressive killers from destroying everybody in the town. As more people die Josh searches for ways to stop the Botbees. Kirstin, Alicia, Ben, Derek led by Josh, actively seek out the Botbees to destroy them before they destroy the town—and the world. Time is of the essence as the swarm continues to grow, but with few resources except their desperation to stop the senseless destruction, Josh and the others have little hope of succeeding.

In the end each one of the group plays a specific part in a plan that Josh has devised, which takes them into the woods near Frieda's clinic. One by one, each goes his separate way following Josh's plan … and one by one each meets a hideous fate, all but Josh.

In the climax Josh must face his nemesis—Max. He's in a cave along with the Botbees which have entered it attracted by spilled Pheromone. Josh fights Max along with having to destroy all the Botbees in the cave. Josh contains and seals all the Botbees inside before making his escape.

... but maybe not all of them ...

THE SIX MOST IMPORTANT SCENES

Before you begin to write your outline, I'd like to review the importance of writing causal scenes. Remember, all of your scenes must be related to one another. One scene should lead into another and originate from the previous scene. For instance, all the scenes in Act I should include those that set up the problem and give information to your audience. In Act II you include all those scenes that create complications and obstacles to prevent your main character from reaching his goal. In Act III all your scenes will lead to the resolution and the climactic scene.

[handwritten: p. 83]

However, to break the script down even further you can also think in terms of the six most important scenes in your structure. These scenes are your guidelines for all scenes that follow.

[handwritten: The 6 scenes are 3. The climax, opening and closing for ACTS 1, 2, 3]

The first scene you should start with is the Climactic scene. Until you know the ending, as I've stated over and over, you can't write your script. After you have determined the ending, the next scene to develop is your opening scene, the scene that sets off your story with a problem to be solved or a goal to be reached.

The other four key scenes are the opening scenes for Act II and Act III, and the last scenes of Act I and Act II. These six scenes are of major importance. They are the blueprint for you to use as you begin to fill in all your other scenes. Knowing this blueprint will make writing your outline very easy. The end of Act I is also known as the 1st Turning Point of your script. It is when the main character can't keep on going as she has been and the action is turned around into Act II, when your character's actions take a new direction.

The last scene at the end of Act II is known as the 2nd Turning Point of your script. Your script is at a high point of drama and again your main character is at a crossroads or turning point. She can't ever go back to the way things used to be. This is the next highest point of drama and leads the main character into Act III, which propels the action into the highest point of drama, known as the Climax and it's the end of Act III.

[handwritten: ✻ AT THE END OF ACT 2: "ALL IS LOST" AND THE SOLUTION DAWNS, IS THE BREAK INTO ACT 3.]

THE FIRST HALF OF ACT 2 IS A FALSE VICTORY. THE SECOND HALF IS A FALSE DEFEAT. THE MIDPOINT BREAK IS THE PROTAGONIST'S POINT OF NO RETURN, HE IS FULLY COMMITTED.

92   CHAPTER 10

To help make your screenplay manageable it's important to understand and be familiar with these major scenes. Another important scene in your screenplay is known as the midpoint. It is in Act II and at the middle of your script, around page 60. In a romantic comedy the midpoint is where the great romance, which was going along smoothly suddenly changes because of obstacles and problems. This is known as the midpoint of the script because it's actually halfway through the screenplay.

THE OUTLINE (1 CARD/SCENE)
THE STEP OUTLINE

An outline is the main blueprint for your work. When you're writing a script you must develop an extensive and complete outline. Scriptwriters must create what is known as the Step Outline. It is a scene outline that describes step-by-step what happens in each scene in a couple of sentences. It shows the order of the scenes and the action that happens in each scene.

The Step Outline is essential to establish the direction of your script and the sequence of your scenes. It really creates the basis of your blueprint for screenwriting, which is vital when structuring your script. With your outline completed, it is an easy task to write your script. It is developing your outline that takes hard work.

1, If you aren't sure how to do an outline, start with writing a Synopsis first as described above. Then begin your outline by starting with the opening scene, then write down one or two sentences that describe the scene. Do this for every scene in a sequential order until you reach the climax or the final scene.

2. Every scene you include must relate to the spine or storyline of your script. The scenes in your outline describe the essence of your material and create the shape or form of your structure. No scene should be included in your structure unless it serves the overall purpose. Setting up your scenes in this manner, helps to develop a fast-moving, workable plot structure.

CARDS There are several ways to develop your Step Outline. Some people like to use 3 × 5 or 5 × 7 cards and write one or two sentences for each scene. Using cards gives you a lot of freedom because you can move them around and change them from one act to the other. Some writers even use different colored cards for each act so they can differentiate between the acts. For example, use blue cards for Act I, pink cards for Act II, and yellow cards for Act III.

You can also take large sheets of paper and divide them into three separate sections so you can see all the scenes at once. Some people use a large bulletin board to set up their scenes and others use the floor to lay out scenes. Whatever method you decide on is a matter of personal choice. The main purpose for your Step Outline is to get your script in the best structure, with each scene moving in a cause-and-effect fashion toward the climax.

I require all my students to create the Step Outline before they put a single word down in script format. This outline is really the most important aspect of story development for the screenwriter. Until your outline works in a tight, straight line, you won't have a blueprint for writing to follow and you won't have a script. Don't try short cuts. Developing an outline in the beginning will save you blood, sweat and tears, plus months of hard work in finding where you are in the story.

THE TREATMENT (20 – 40 pages)

The story prose w/o dialogue, showing.

A treatment usually consists of between 20 to 40 pages, typewritten and double spaced. It is a step-by-step detailed narrative account of your story written in present tense prose. It should include every scene you have written. Many people write a treatment only after they have developed a step outline. The treatment is an expanded version of your outline and it is written in exciting prose, detailing everything that happens in your script. A good, solid treatment could be shot into a film, since it includes all the action in a film. The only thing it doesn't include is the dialogue.

Take time to create an interesting, well-written treatment, that will hold the readers interest and excite them. When you write your treatment don't explain or tell your readers what's happening. Show them what's happening through writing the external action that takes place. Use the best prose you can, by having concrete verbs and action words and limiting your adjectives and adverbs. Show, don't tell.

Remember your prose must translate into film. Write visually. Picture each scene before you begin to write it and translate these visual images into descriptive words. Sometimes writers are asked to develop a treatment, before they write a script. It is often on the strength of your treatment that you'll sell or not sell your screenplay. Don't let it be filled with weak verbs, adjectives or adverbs. Make your story come alive!!

Keep the action going through the use of strong verbs and visual images. Don't give camera directions in the treatment or it won't be a good read. If an executive doesn't like your treatment, he certainly won't ask you to write the script. Be certain you have a well-written, structured treatment that will intrigue, excite, and interest your reader.

BLUEPRINT FOR SCREENWRITING

1. Write a synopsis first before you do a step outline. Remember *p 89* it is written in prose and it's the broad strokes of your outline.
2. Develop a step outline and state the purpose of each scene in a couple sentences. *p. 87*
3. Does each scene relate to your story-line? If yes, how can you be sure? *If you remove a scene, the story falls apart.*
4. Develop your blueprint for screen writing by creating an extensive outline for your work.
5. Turn your step outline into a treatment. Does it read well? Could your treatment be translated into film?
6. Add dialogue where you can't show the story with action, p. 106.
7. From your step outline, create headers and scene narrative in FINAL DRAFT.
8. Then add dialogue where you can't show the story with action narrative, p. 106-113.
   a. To keep a character's voice, write all of the character's dialogue at once. Do the same with the next character, etc. Do not jump back & forth between characters or you'll loose the characters dialect or voice.

Chapter 11

Script Format

"Get black on white."

—Guy de Maupassant

When you submit a script to an agent, movie company or network, it must be written in script format. The first sign of an amateur is when he or she submits a script with the improper format. In a script there are basic rudiments, specific number of pages, certain line spacing for your script format.

Your script format is a blueprint developed by you that demonstrates to other people what's being seen and heard. It includes the dialogue, the description of characters and location of the shots and directions for the characters' actions. This format is totally different from any other type of fictional writing and prose.

You should never submit any script unless you know the rules for script format. That is one rule that must never be broken. It is essential that you have the correct format or your script won't even get read. Your script should read like any well-written piece of writing. Make it flow and involve the reader, so he or she won't want to put it down.

One way to ensure the smooth flow of work is not to include camera angles and directions. You are the writer. Let the director or the cameraman decide on the camera shots and angles they want to use. If you include camera angles it will lessen the impact of your story and slow down the action of your script. It will distract your reader rather than attract him to want to continue reading.

There are terrific computer programs such as Final Draft or Movie Magic Screenwriter that will format your screenplay in a professional manner. These programs make it easy for you to correctly format your script without being bogged down in worrying about margins and style. If you don't have these programs the following example is the standard for formatting. Here are the correct script format specifications:

At the opening of your script put the words FADE IN: written in *FADE IN* capital letters, which is referred to as CAPS. It is positioned in the *CAPS* upper left hand corner of your page. It means curtain rises. At the end of your script type the words FADE OUT: in the lower right *FADE OUT* hand corner of your page. It is also in caps and means fade to black. These are the only times you ever use these terms. After writing FADE IN: skip two lines and write whether the shot will be an inside or outside shot; the location being shot; and the time of day or night. *SLUGLINE*

This is referred to as the SLUGLINE. It's written in all caps and *INT.* introduces each new scene. Write INT. for interior shot, EXT. for ex- *EXT* terior shot, the location and the time. For example:

INT. RESTAURANT—DAY or EXT. STREET—NIGHT

These are written in caps and are always used to indicate when there is a new location and starting a new shot. After the slugline double space and begin to write the necessary description of the res- *description* taurant or the street. Only write the essential description that will be shot by the cameraman. Don't write a lot of description, but use an economy of words, describing just what must be seen. The description or directions are written in single space, upper and lower case, just like sentence structure.

Besides description you also write the action in the same way, in *prose* upper and lower case and in prose, with active-verbs, short and to the point. Use the best type of prose you can write. When you introduce a character for the first time, always use capital letters for the first and last name and a brief description of the character. "SALLY JOHNS, early 30's, blond hair, and beautiful smile," could be enough description. Don't get too detailed with a character's description unless it is necessary for your story to have a specific type of character.

dialogue

The dialogue is written in upper and lower case directly under the character's name. It is centered below the characters name from 35–65.

parenthetical

Parenthetical is written in lower case in parenthesis and places beneath the character's name, on a line that's separate form the dialogue. In the directions always capitalize any camera shots or sound effects.

Some other directions you need to know are the following:

P.O.V. (Point of View) If you want to have a shot from the same perspective a character is seeing it, write SUSAN'S P.O.V. The camera is behind the character and sees what the character sees.

V.O. (Voice Over) is used when you hear a character's voice but you don't see him. This is used a lot when one character talks on the phone and we hear the voice over the phone but don't see the other character. It is also used when someone is talking over a scene that is being shot, but the character talking is not in the scene. When you see shots of a car traveling down the highway and you hear a voice narrating over the scene, that is considered a voice over.

O.S. (Off Screen) is used in the directions when we hear a sound coming from another room. It could be written in caps as the following: O.S. MUSIC FROM RADIO or O.S. SLAMMING OF CAR DOOR.

B.G. (Background) is usually part of the description.

Transitions include CUT TO:, DISSOLVE TO:, MATCH CUT TO:. They are justified on the right margin, and are written all in caps. Use with discretion, because a it is obvious when you start a new scene, since you have a slugline such as:

INT. OFFICE—DAY.

CUT TO: is used at the end of a scene when you want to quickly cut from one scene to another.

DISSOLVE TO: is used at the end of a scene when you want a slow change from one place to another.

MATCH CUT TO: is used when you are showing a person or object and you suddenly have the same person or object, but you cut to a different scene.

INSERT is used when you need to show a close-up of an object inserted into the scene. Insert is used a lot in mysteries to plant a clue or red herring.

If you are using a computer the outer margins of your script are 15 and 75. Use these margins to write your description and your directions. Action scenes are long descriptions of what your characters are doing. When you're ready to have a character speak, double space and capitalize the character's name and center it in the middle of the page at 45 margin. Write the dialogue directly under the name and centered at 35 to 65. Any directions written in the dialogue are centered at 40 with parenthesis around the directions (angry). When you want to write more description or longer directions, double space and write it from margin to margin (15 to 75).

THE BUSINESS OR EXPOSITION

The description and action are also known as the business of your script. The business includes all the characters' actions and the descriptions of all the settings. Writing the business of your script is important to keep exciting and interesting. If it is too long and boring, you'll lose the reader's interest. This is not the time to try your hand at writing a novel. Don't use an excess of words. Write what is necessary and make it sound exciting by your careful choice of words. You need to keep the business short and to the point.

Don't use elaborate explanations or descriptions. Just write what you want to be visual. Save the flowery descriptions for other writing. Just be direct and precise when describing the action, eliminating adverbs and adjectives as much as possible. Make your writing active and your words specific.

Use the best prose possible for your directions, since your business must translate into film. Let the words sing on the page and the descriptions be visual and concrete, because your script will first be read before it's seen. You want it to be a good read to keep people who are reading your script interested in knowing what's going to happen next.

The directions never tell what a character is THINKING OR FEELING, only what the character is DOING. Nothing else should be included. Don't depend on directions or lengthy explanations to carry your script. Only use directions when absolutely necessary. Remember, you're not writing a novel.

You are writing a blueprint for cinematographers to film, actors to act, directors to director, film editors to edit, and so on. This is a collaborative effort and you, the writer are the Creator of it all. Make your blueprint clear, concise and visually exciting.

I have included an example of a scene written in script format. The scene has only one purpose and has a beginning, a middle and a climax. From now on write your scenes using the correct script format.

EXAMPLE OF SCRIPT FORMAT

This example of script format doesn't contain any camera angles and very little adjectives or adverbs.

This is how all scenes for your screenplay should be written. You also use this format for a television movie, except you need more act breaks.

FADE IN:

INT. HOSPITAL—DAY

NANCY WINTERS, 42 attractive brunette is wearing a hospital gown. She walks toward a table, which has a bottle of champagne on it and takes a glass. She fills up the glass with champagne.

NANCY
Let's have another drink. As long as
I'm breaking the rules, I want to
enjoy myself.

MICHAEL WINTERS, 45, slightly built looks at her. He needs a shave and has a worried look on his face.

MICHAEL
Do you think you should have any
more?

> NANCY
> Why not. If I get drunk you won't
> have to worry about putting me to
> bed will you?

She holds her glass in her hand and pours some more wine. Her hand shakes and it spills as she pours it. She quickly gulps it down. Michael gets up and tries to take the glass from her. She pushes him away.

> NANCY (CONT'D.)
> (yelling)
> Leave me alone!

Michael walks to a chair and sits down. He picks up the newspaper and begins reading.

> NANCY (CONT'D.)
> I'm sorry. It's just that I'm so
> nervous. Tell me again what the
> doctor told you.

> MICHAEL
> I already told you. How many times
> do I have to say it.

> NANCY
> Please, just once more.

Michael doesn't look at her while he speaks.

> MICHAEL
> He said there's nothing to worry
> about. It's just minor surgery. You'll
> be fine, just fine.

> NANCY
> Are you certain that's all? Look at
> me.

Michael turns to face her.

> MICHAEL
> Yes, I'm sure.

Nancy goes to the bottle and pours herself another full glass. She
smiles as she takes a long gulp.

NANCY

I'll drink to that. (takes a sip)

When I'm out of here, let's go on a
trip. What about that cross country
trip we never took?

Michael continues reading the newspaper. He looks up at Nancy.

MICHAEL

Sure, sure that sounds just great.

He resumes his reading while Nancy continues looking at him

NANCY

Or maybe we can take that cruise we
always planned. What do you think?

Michael doesn't respond.

NANCY (cont'd.)

Or else we could use the money to
redecorate the house and forget the
trips entirely. (beat) But you always
wanted to take a Safari to Africa,
and I know I'd be up to it in a few
weeks. Right? Michael? What do you
think?

MICHAEL

Sounds great.

NANCY

Which one? The trip here in the
states or in Africa?

MICHAEL

Either. Whatever one you want.

She looks at him.

> NANCY
> Are you sure you're telling me
> everything he said?

> MICHAEL
> Believe me! I told you everything.

He gets up and walks to her. He puts his arms around her.

Nancy leans in his arms and rests her head on his shoulder.

> NANCY
> I'm sorry. I know everything will be
> just fine. I'm just a worry wart.

> MICHAEL
> As if I didn't know.

He takes his hand and messes up her hair, turns and quickly walks
back to the chair. He sits down.

> NANCY
> Michael, why did I have to sign that
> release?

> MICHAEL
> (Casually)
> That's just routine. Say, guess who
> sent you candy? The Wagners. I
> have the mail. Look at all these
> cards!

He reaches in his pocket and takes out a bundle of cards. He gets
up and starts to hand them to Nancy, but she covers her eyes and
begins to SOB. The cards fall to the floor.

> NANCY
> I should have been home by now.
> God, I thought all the tests were
> negative. Why more surgery? Don't
> lie to me, Michael, please.
> (beat)
> Michael, I'm so scared.

Nancy collapses on the bed face down and continues SOBBING. Michael looks away and quickly wipes his eyes. He rushes to her and pats her on the back.

                    MICHAEL
          You'll be fine. The doctor just has to
          satisfy himself that all the
          surrounding tissue is clean. That's all
          there is to it.

                    NANCY
               (hopefully)
          You wouldn't lie to me, Michael.
          You'd tell me the truth wouldn't you?

Michael starts to rub her shoulder and takes a handkerchief and dries her tears as he turns her around to face him.

                    MICHAEL
          Of course, I'd tell you the truth. You
          know I would. I love you. Now dry
          your eyes and let's have another
          glass of wine.

                    NANCY
          To the future ... together.

She looks him in the eyes as they click their glasses together.

                                        FADE OUT:

BLUEPRINT FOR SCREENWRITING

1. Write a scene using script format.
2. Write an action scene without using any dialogue.
3. Write a scene including the following directions:
   (a) P.O.V.   (b) V.O.   (c) O.S.
4. Write a scene using NO camera directions.
5. What is a slugline? Write one.
6. What does match cut mean? Give an example.

Chapter 12

Dialogue

"The difference between the right word and the almost right word is the difference between lightning and the lightning bug."

—Mark Twain

Because film is visual, it is much better to SHOW than to TELL. Never use dialogue in place of action. After all, the first movies were silent with no dialogue. And look how successful they were. So when do you use dialogue? You use dialogue when you can't show what you want through action. Your dialogue needs to accomplish one of three things:

1. Give information
2. Move your story forward
3. Reveal character

If your dialogue doesn't fit into any of these categories, don't use it! Never write dialogue just for the sake of having small talk or exchanging pleasantries, like "Hi," "How are you?" "I'm fine." These pleasantries will slow down your screenplay and are boring. There is no purpose for small talk, and all dialogue must have a purpose.

KEEP IT SHORT AND SIMPLE

Don't slow down your screenplay by writing dialogue that is filled with directions. Avoid adjectives and adverbs like (happily), (sadly), (angrily), (fearfully), except when there is uncertainty of your intention. Otherwise, let the director or actor decide how to say their lines. Don't play director and try to tell the actor how to say a line of dialogue. It is an insult to the professional actor and a sure sign that you're a novice.

The shorter your dialogue the better. Use short speeches and crisp dialogue. Pace your short speeches with longer speeches. Use interruptions and pauses interspersed throughout your dialogue. The biggest mistake beginning screenwriters make is having the characters give long-winded speeches that end up sounding like monologues.

Silence can be more impactful and emotional than extensive dialogue and explanations. In real life we communicate nonverbally much more than we use verbal communication. Keep in mind when writing dialogue your character's tone of voice, facial expression, and eye contact. Close your eyes and visualize what emotion you want your character to express before you write the dialogue.

Instead of using words, try to communicate your character's feelings through a gesture, facial expression, or body movement. Use these actions in place of dialogue.

All the Dialogue Sounds the Same

One of the greatest stumbling blocks to all writers—having the same sounding voice for all the characters. But first let me address the issue of why this is so common to all writers.

I firmly believe the writer is all of the characters, and the dialogue the characters speak is really the author's voice and what he or she wants to say through them. This is all well and good if writers are able to reveal who they are, but the problem occurs when writers use only the one voice and are afraid to reach inside to all the different voices.

I've encountered this dialogue problem in every writing class. Most writers can't get their characters to sound original with their own strong voice because writers can't connect to all of their own voices. This makes all the major characters end up sounding the same, and usually they all sound like the voice of the writer.

This is such a pervasive problem that I'm presently working with writers individually and in groups to specifically target this issue. Recently, I worked with a successful screenwriter with many produced credits, who was under contract to write her first feature.

When she turned in her screenplay the reception to it was negative, the major complaint being that every character in her screenplay sounded exactly like the main character—dull and boring. She finally overcame her screenplay problem by working on the voices from inside her and letting them come out and express themselves.

All the Characters Sound the Same

In addition to all the dialogue sounding the same, the next common problem with dialogue is there seems to be no differentiation between each character's style of speech. The writers don't seem to care whether or not the character is a society matron, a waitress, a gangster, a teenager, educated, illiterate, southern or northern. They make the dialogue sound alike for all of them.

Your dialogue should not be interchangeable among your various characters. Before you write dialogue get inside your character and listen to him talk. If he's a teenager in the 21st century, he'll speak different from a teenager living in the 1960s. If you're writing about a modern day teenager, observe teenagers at their local hangouts or their school, so you can describe the slang and their special "in talk." Don't make a society matron sound like a prostitute. Decide what kind of dialogue you need to fit your specific character, then make it sound appropriate for that character.

Less Is More

The third most common mistake when writing dialogue is everyone usually writes monologues or long-winded speeches. When writing dialogue remember: Less is more! Make each word count by avoiding all the meaningless chit-chat. And realize that people talk with interruptions, with hesitations, in monosyllables, with grunts, "er's," "oh's," "ah's," sighs and pauses.

In reality people are usually so busy thinking about what they want to say, they rarely wait long enough to let the other person finish speaking. And when they finally speak, what they say very often has nothing to do with what has just been said. One person may begin talking about a subject, while the other person doesn't respond to what was said, but will start going on his or her own tangent.

Pay attention to the way people converse in your daily life. Become a listener, as difficult as that may be. Stop, look and listen! The only way to make your dialogue sound realistic is to listen to people talking wherever you are and note it in your writer's journal. By doing this you will raise your awareness to how people really talk and mostly how people don't listen!

In writing dialogue you want to give each character a unique voice to keep them from all sounding the same. One approach to finding a voice for your character is an external one. If you're having quite a bit of trouble getting into your character's head, try to discover his or her voice from your memory, thinking of a particular person or a composite of several people from your past who remind you of this character.

Make the Dialogue Fit the Characters

Then find the best adjective you can for this character. What word best describes his or her overall personality? If you've already chosen the best adjective from the assignment in a previous chapter, then take the adjective and think in terms of dialogue. If the adjective you chose was arrogant, then make the dialogue alive with arrogant phrases and rejoinders.

Maybe you have words like "charming, surface, smooth, friendly, glib." Although these words all sound similar, each adjective represents a special characteristic, which would then become dominant with that character's voice and that attitude would express itself through the dialogue. But don't make all your characters sound glib. Use this attitude for just a specific character.

After you've settled on the best description then go into your past and think of someone you know who is similar to this character or who resembles some aspect of his or her personality. Concentrate on how he or she walks, mannerisms, behaviors, gestures and the way he or she communicates. What does the character sound like when he or she speaks? Is the voice melodious, does he or she speak quickly, make eye contact when speaking? Does the character talk in a booming voice or whisper? What are the rhythms of his or her words? Once you answer all of these questions and others you'll start to quiet your own voice from the character's and begin to give him or her a "voice that will ring true," to the character.

One of the assignments I've given my students is to listen to people talking, and to overhear as many conversations as they can in banks, restaurants, on the bus, at work, in bars, anywhere at all. You can do the same by using your life situations as an opportunity to master the craft of realistic dialogue.

After completing the assignment they discovered that people don't talk in long speeches. They don't get the chance. In fact, most people love to talk about themselves more than anything or anyone else, so they can't wait for the other person to finish speaking before they interrupt them.

Dialogue should create emotional conflict between your characters and develop tension between them that leads to some new action being taken on the part of your characters. Dialogue must be dramatic. It is best used when it creates arguments, fights, and explosions of emotion between your characters. When you write dialogue, always create conflict and tension, and you'll never lose your audience's interest.

EXPOSITION

(The business or action in a screenplay)

Exposition is the act of writing necessary information to the audience, so they can understand the purpose of your story. It is vital to give them specific information so they'll know what your story is about. This helps your audience become involved and stay interested because they know what's happening. It is often referred to as the business—or the action in a screenplay.

In the first ten minutes of any film you must give your audience information on what the film is about and who the main character is. Your craft as a writer is to keep your audience from walking out of the theater or turning off the television, while getting this information. And the information needs to flow and not be intrusive, but written as part of the screenplay, so it doesn't seem as if you're lecturing your audience.

Years ago, plays would often open with two servants discussing all the terrible things that had happened to the master or mistress of the manor. Obviously, this method is unacceptable and certainly dated. You don't want to use the greek chorus to tell the audience about your screenplay. Avoid other cliched methods of giving information. Be creative when you write exposition. Let your mind flow and think of unique and clever ways to give your audience vital and necessary information without being boring. *How to do it*

How do you write exposition in a way that won't lose your audience? You write it with conflict and dramatic action. This way your audience isn't aware you're giving them a lot of information. Let your characters discuss a problem, while racing a car or making love, which allows your audience to get the facts they need to know without being obvious.

Emotional Dialogue

Put emotional intensity into your exposition while you relate the pertinent information. Give information during times of crisis, for example, when a teenager is arrested, a woman is revealed as a thief, or a man loses his job. Whatever you do, don't have your exposition sound like a lecture. Make it so dramatic and interesting your audience won't even be aware they are receiving information. *Expls. How to do it 1, 2.*

Examples of films with fabulous dialogue are *American Beauty*, *Kissing Jessica Stein*, and *Sylvia*. The dialogue comes from the characters and reflects their personalities. It also reveals the characters and moves the story forward. In these films, when information is given, it is done in such a unique way that the dialogue seems natural and interesting.

Today in the entertainment industry, writers are more concerned with their screenplay being a good "read" more than they were in the past. This means the rules aren't quite as rigid and much of their exposition is more personal. In fact, in a recent screenplay that was bought for over a million dollars, the writer refers to a love scene as being "so hot that it would shock my mother." *Bending the rules*

Practice listening to people speaking wherever you go. Train your ear for accents and dialects. Become an observer of people as they *Summary Tips 1, 2,* talk, so you can learn how to use mannerisms and gestures with your dialogue. Make your dialogue dramatic when giving vital information. And most of all, be sure you have no unnecessary words, keep your dialogue to the point, and filled with conflict. Use strong verbs in your exposition and make your sentences speak out with power.

BLUEPRINT FOR SCREENWRITING

1. Write a scene using exposition, but make it exciting.
2. Write a scene of emotional conflict by using just dialogue.
3. Listen to people talking whenever you are in public places.
4. Record the conversations in a notebook.
5. Write a scene based on an overhead conversation. Make it dramatic.
6. Record your dialogue into a tape recorder. Does it sound conversational or like a monologue?
7. Write a scene using different character types and make each speech pattern unique and distinct.
8. Write a scene using only monosyllables and nothing else. Do you have conflict and tension?

Chapter 13

Subtext

[handwritten: Subtext is the way to make your writing more dramatic and emotionally powerful, 122. It is the best type of writing, 114.]

"Talking about oneself can also be a means to conceal oneself."
—Frederich Nietzche

[handwritten margin note: Def.]

All good writing contains subtext. Subtext is the unspoken feelings that hide beneath the words. It is that which is unsaid and is the best type of writing you can write. Think of all the situations you have at work and home. How many times do you NOT say what you want to say to your boss, your friends, your parents, your children? I'm sure you do it more often than you'd like to admit.

[handwritten margin note: SOAPS w/oct SUBTEXT, Too on-the-nose.]

Soap opera and melodramas are examples of writing without the use of subtext. The characters just say everything that's on their mind. They are up front with their feelings and let it "all hang out." For example, a soap opera character might say, "Oh, I'm going to kill myself now that Charles has left me for that young hussy," or "Life isn't worth living now that Sue is gone." Subtext is the opposite of this type of writing.

EMOTIONS BENEATH THE WORDS

Because dialogue has to be emotional rather than conversational, one of the best ways of writing dialogue is by using subtext. Subtext

[handwritten: When text is too "on-the-nose," you fix it with subtext and action that shows the characters' true feelings as in the example on p 115.]

provides you with the tools to allow your audience to identify with
your characters.

Expl

Suppose a man and his girlfriend have been living together for
five years and he's really getting bored with the relationship. Let's
say he wants to get out of it, but doesn't know what to do and feels
trapped. In obvious, direct text he might voice those exact senti-
ments: "I'm really sick and tired of this relationship and I want out."
There's no room for doubt and no room to imagine anything else
that might be going on with him. He's just saying what he feels, with
no mystery at all.

In subtext that same situation would be dealt with quite differently. Let's say he's just come home from the office for dinner. He
slams the door. He then ignores his girl friend while she's talking to
him. Perhaps he gives her a grunt or two when she asks him a question. During dinner he hides behind his newspaper, while she continues making small talk about her day.

This keeps up until he suddenly explodes, "Where did you buy
this piece of shoe leather?" He pushes his plate away. "Can't you do
anything right?" he yells as he jumps up from the table, knocking
over his chair.

"Well, if you don't like it, make dinner yourself," she replies.

"Maybe I will," he threatens.

"Why don't you find a maid or someone else who cooks better?"
she screams.

"That's not a bad idea," he shouts, putting on his coat and hat
and heading for the door. "Don't wait up," he says as he slams the
door after him.

That is subtext! The man and woman are really not arguing about
food. He wants out, he's feeling desperate. She is feeling bewildered,
hurt and threatened. Maybe he has another woman? Maybe he
doesn't love her anymore? But do they talk about their relationship—her fears, his wanting out? No! They talk about cooking!

When to Use Subtext

Viewers watching this scene are able to bring their own life experiences into it and identify with the characters. Haven't we all felt the
pain of being rejected? Haven't we all felt the uneasiness of trying to *Something,*

* Use subtext when a character is trying to hide,
avoid something, or conceil embarassment;

end a relationship and not knowing how? Of course we have! In fact, in most of our daily contacts we use subtext, especially when emotions and feelings are involved.

If you think about your daily life, you'll realize what an important part subtext plays in it. Do you tell your boss to "go to hell" when he asks you to stay overtime? I don't think you do, not if you want to be employed. But you might go to your desk and start slamming papers around or furiously sharpen your pencils. You are using subtext in your actions!

In personal relationships you probably use subtext more than you use text. If you always said exactly what you felt, you'd probably end up without any friends, family or lovers. I give my students the following analogy about subtext:

"You use subtext when you're dating, and text when you're married."

Most of us go through life NOT saying how we really feel. We hide our feelings behind our masks and we behave in ways that are different from our feelings. Think about those emotionally charged situations that you have experienced throughout your life—births, deaths, illness, accidents, weddings, break-ups, divorces. At these highly emotional times, most of us are at a loss for words, and our feelings remain buried deep inside us.

Then there are the social situations, when you want to make a good impression: asking a person out on a date, wanting to make-out with your date, meeting someone you like at a party, a bar, a dance, trying to join a social club, a fraternity, or organization. At these times do you say what's on your mind and behave exactly as you wish? Or do you act in a way you think would create a good impression? Of course, you don't say what you really feel. If you said and did exactly what you wanted to, you'd probably get knocked down, beaten up, or slapped in the face.

People put on a false front most of the time. They live behind their mask or their facade. They behave not as they really feel, but how they want to appear to others. This is not deception, this is self-preservation, and survival. It is how most of us act in our lives. We do this for self-protection, for our self-esteem and for our ego-strength.

Many writers experience a lot of difficulty when trying to write subtext. Instead of writing subtext they often use double entendres, saying something which has a double meaning, or they write dialogue with one character being sarcastic to another. That is not subtext. It is just people being sarcastic!

Subtext—What You Don't Say — *is What the Scene is Really About*

Every good film is loaded with subtext. It is subtle, and more than sarcasm or small talk. When you write subtext there is always much more going on in a scene than meets the eye. Subtext is the emotional feeling beneath the words. It is the truth beneath what is being said and heard. Subtext is what the scene really is about.

The sample scene in the chapter on screenplay format is filled with subtext. The man and his wife never once mention the fact that she is dying. They talk around it, and make plans for a future trip. Neither speak about what each one fears the most. This scene between the husband and wife is much more dramatic and emotional than if either spoke about her illness and how scared they both feel.

Subtext is when the audience feels and knows there is much more going on in a scene than what is being said and done. When you write a scene in subtext you doubt what the characters are really saying, because you know they are feeling something different from the way they're behaving. *They reveal their true feelings by what they do*

Another example of subtext has to do with relationships. As you know, at the beginning of every romantic relationship the two people involved put their best foot forward. They present themselves in the best possible manner, since they want to be perceived in a positive way. They might be bored to tears with the conversation, but do they show their boredom? No! They smile, ask questions, make jokes, and show interest in what's being said in the moment.

But beneath their small talk they are feeling another way. Maybe they are wondering if they're making a good impression, or if their date will want to see them again. Maybe they're afraid their last remark sounded stupid. Perhaps one wants to end up at her date's apartment later in the evening. Maybe he can't wait to get home alone. But do they tell each other how they're feeling? Of course not. They're saying one thing but feeling another.

Think of your own dating experiences. How many times did you tell your date how you really felt, especially those times when you were either disappointed and couldn't wait for your date to end. Or other times when you were so smitten that you felt tongue-tied and awkward. In either case you tried to hide your true feelings, so you wouldn't hurt the other person or you wouldn't allow yourself to be vulnerable.

That is when you acted one way but felt another. Well, in good screenwriting that's how your characters act too. In fact in great screenplays there usually is little dialogue, but a lot of feelings beneath the words. It's important for you to use as much subtext in your character's dialogue or their actions. This allows your audience to bring their own feelings into play and enables them to identify with your characters.

"ANNIE HALL" EXPL.

In Woody Allen's classic film *Annie Hall*, there is a brilliant scene between Annie Hall played by Diane Keaton and Alvy Singer, played by Woody Allen, when they have just met for the first time in their relationship. How do they act? They make small talk to each other and both are really saying nothing. As they are talking, subtitles are being flashed on the screen revealing what they are really thinking. This shows the true meaning of subtext. They are saying things to impress and feeling stupid about what they say. It is truly a terrific example of how characters and people behave when they want to make a good impression, but feel stupid inside.

Subtext in Actions

Subtext is how you want to write, especially when your characters are feeling emotional. For example, since most of us act one way and feel another, you want to write subtext in your characters' actions as well as their dialogue. Subtext often is shown through a character's behavior. A wonderful example of revealing subtext is through a character's actions, when he or she is behaving one way but feeling another as in *Ordinary People*. This film by Alvin Sargeant, which is based on the novel by Judith Guest is one of the best films to demonstrate the power of subtext.

"ORDINARY PEOPLE" EXPL

In a scene in the film the mother, Beth, on the surface, says and does all the right things to her son, Conrad. However, it is clear to the audience that she's feeling different from the way she's speaking and behaving. She isn't being real, but playing a part. She is the perfect wife and mother but beneath her mask she is an imperfect person, unable to really give love.

One of the best examples of subtext in the movie is when the family is gathered together at Thanksgiving and they are taking pictures. The father wants to take a picture of Conrad and his mother together. All the while Beth keeps smiling as she refuses and keeps insisting to her husband, Cal, that she wants to take his picture with Conrad. As this continues Conrad finally moves away from his mother and shouts, "Forget the goddamn picture."

This is an excellent example of a scene that has strong emotions beneath what is really happening. This scene has much more going on among the characters than just taking a family photograph. In fact, it is a pivotal scene for Conrad, because it's the first time he is able to be honest and show his frustration, hurt, and anger toward his mother. The scene really is one of the most emotional scenes in the film and one which certainly is an impetus for a change in the family dynamics.

In *American Beauty*, a film about the modern American family and their values, there is a marvelous example of subtext between the father, the mother and the daughter when we see them at the dining room having dinner together. There are layers of emotions going on in that scene besides eating dinner. It is obvious that each family member is feeling many different emotions toward one another than is being expressed.

Each one feels isolated, lonely and disconnected from the other family members. Everyone is wearing a protective mask. Somehow we know that this family is on the verge of falling apart. We feel uncomfortable watching this scene and how the characters are hiding their real feelings. This is a truly great scene filled with emotional tension. It has so much more going on beneath the surface than having dinner. The family is ready to disintegrate!

Actions Speak Louder Than Words

People often act pleasant and smile, when talking to another person, but what they are saying is really cutting and hurts the other person. Haven't you seen people feeling sad, yet they are smiling? Subtext can be used with people acting differently from what they're feeling. "Pretend your happy when you're blue," is a line from a song, which illustrates how most of us live.

2-WAY SUBTEXT

In fact, this is how your characters should behave in your script. When you write subtext in your screenplay you may either involve both characters who know what's really going on, but neither is being honest. You could say they both are playing a role to avoid being hurt. A good example of this could be when you're writing about a

Expl.

romantic relationship which is about to end. "It isn't you, it's me," is a great line of subtext, when the one who's breaking up tries not to hurt the other.

ONE-WAY SUBTEXT

You also may use subtext involving only just one character, while the other has no idea what's really going on. Let's say a man has just gotten fired from his job. He comes home to his wife and family but

Expl.

doesn't say a word about getting fired. However, he just begins yelling at his kids to put away their toys. Then he starts an argument with his wife about her being a terrible housekeeper. Finally, he kicks the dog.

This is an example of a character acting one way but feeling another. He's taking out his frustration at losing his job on his family and his dog. His wife and his children don't know what's really going on with him. He probably feels ashamed, low self-esteem and fear about how he's going to support his family. But he's the only one who knows the real reason he's behaving in such a mean way. He's the only one involved with the subtext of his actions and words, since nobody else is aware he was fired. Subtext is the undercurrent behind his actions and words. It is the emotional truth he's really feeling underneath his surface, ranging from fear, guilt and insecurity.

Most of us hide who we really are behind our masks, especially when it comes from our need to survive. We learn how to hide our real feelings when we are children. Our feelings go underground and we live in subtext just to get along in school, at home and with friends.

Expressing Your Feelings Through Subtext

I've coached thousands of writers who didn't know what they were feeling, because they were so used to hiding their real emotions behind their masks. Many writers aren't able to find their true voice when they want to create scripts with emotional depth. I've helped these writers discover their authentic voice by giving them permission to make their writing truthful and unique.

Most of them were never allowed to express their feelings when they were small children. They hid the real little person inside and became the child their parents forced them to be. Many suppressed their anger, sadness, rage, sexual desires and the feelings their parents didn't permit them to express. Now, when these same individuals wanted to give their characters depth, they weren't able to, because they couldn't give to their fictional characters the emotions they couldn't give to themselves.

My goal in working with them was to get them to reach inside and start reconnecting with their repressed feelings. We worked together on their writing about peak emotional experiences in childhood which they recalled. As they emotionally re-experienced their past, these writers eventually learn to honor the truth of what they were feeling and released pent-up passions.

Remarkably they soon were able to put their feelings into their characters and their writing became rich, emotional and deep. Their characters jumped off the page and their dialogue was snappy and filled with emotional undertones and personal feelings.

You can achieve the same wonderful results for your characters and write scenes which are rich in subtext. Remember, when you write your screenplay that you are the creator of your characters and their world. If you can't reach your feelings or express your emotions than you're unable to allow your characters to express them. *How to*

Another way to access what you're really feeling beneath your fa- *notice* cade is to go through your day and make notes in your journal every *subtext* time you say something, but it's not what you really mean. Jot down when you behave a particular way but it's not how you really want to act. Notice how many times a day you don't say anything when you really want to and don't do what you really want to do.

Being aware of what an actor you really are will help you learn to write subtext, especially as you recognize the feelings beneath your words. If you can use subtext in every scene you'll achieve the best type of dramatic writing you can possibly write. Your audience with be able to identify with your characters.

Def Subtext 114

By using subtext you'll also give your audience room to inject their own feelings into the scene. Writing subtext takes time and effort to learn. It isn't easy, but then anything of value isn't easy to achieve. Fight for writing subtext and keep trying until you're able to do it. When you've mastered it the impact of your screenwriting will be more dramatic and emotionally powerful.

BLUEPRINT FOR SCREENWRITING

1. Write a scene using only text.
2. Write the same scene using subtext.
3. Write subtext using actions as well as dialogue.
4. Write a scene having one character use subtext and the other character not.
5. When do you use subtext in your family?
6. What person do you use subtext with at work?
7. On what occasions do you wear your mask? Explain.
8. Write a scene where both characters are using subtext.
9. Notice how many times a day you don't say anything when you really want to and don't do what you really want to do. 121

Chapter 14

Writing From Your Inner Cast of Characters

"All the world's a stage, and all the men and women merely players. They have their exits and their entrances, And one man in his time plays many parts ...."

—William Shakespeare

Every successful writer knows that dynamic characters and meaningful stories come from the inner self. It is my belief that all quality writing must connect to the writer's "inner cast of characters and stories." Any one can learn structure, but it is never craft alone that makes a script outstanding and original. For those of you who want to be more than a craft person in your writing, you need to have ready access to your inner cast of characters. You have to be aware of your own psychology and your inner world—your hopes, fears, joys, dreams and needs. You can't give anything to your characters that you can't give to yourself.

Too often well-structured scripts end up without having any passion, spirit, truth or soul. The secret to having your script stand out from all the rest is to learn how to put "heart" into your characters and "soul" into your writing. Let who you are be expressed through your characters. Let what you want be the goals in your script.

To create characters who experience personal and emotional growth (the goal for all characters) you must infuse them with your own feelings. Unfortunately, most of us can't reach these powerful memories and stories inside, because we have developed defense mechanisms in the guise of protective masks, that we wear all the time. Hiding behind our masks keeps us alienated from our inner selves and becomes our disguise.

Just like these lines from an excerpt of a poem by Dr. Charles M. Galloway suggest: "Don't be fooled by the face I wear ... I wear a thousand masks, that I'm afraid to take off; and none of them are me ...."

Basically, by the time we're five years old we wear our masks to keep us from feeling intense pain, vulnerability and embarrassment. We've been made fun of by our peers, reprimanded by teachers, disciplined by our parents and family, and we soon learn to put on our protective mask to conceal the person we really are. We pretend not to be vulnerable or at least not to show it. But the price we often pay is that we lose our creativity, spontaneity, the prime sources of our real spirit.

WHO AM I?

From once being spontaneous and free we eventually hide our true self, as we discover different roles to play, to keep us from getting hurt. Can you answer the question, "Who Am I?" including all the roles you play in your life: mother, father, sister, uncle, cousin, baseball player, Italian, middle-class, Asian, musician, teacher, child, son, cook, Democrat, letter-writers, Latino, writer, Republican, doctor, homemaker, producer, lover, student, etc.

Get the idea? Now keep writing about all the roles you play in every aspect of your life. After you've completed your list try to separate yourself from your roles. How many of you can't do that? How many of you don't know who you are without your roles?

Now answer the question "Who Am I?" but this time don't list ANY roles you play. Just answer who you are WITHOUT your roles. Who are you inside? Can you answer this question or are you having a difficult time? Could it be you have no idea who you are without your roles or without the masks you wear?

To become a deeper writer you must learn how to separate yourself from the roles you play in life, work, family. To be closed-off emotionally is to fail as a writer and as a human being.

Now ask this same question of your character when you are creating his psychological make-up: "Who am I?" What are the roles your character plays? Is he a lawyer, a doctor, a clerk, a father, a husband, a lover, a son, a brother, a criminal, an atheist, an athlete, a cousin, a scientist, a child, etc.

Next, answer the question of your character: "Who Am I?" without the roles? What are his values? What is his belief system? Do you know the answers? Do you know what your values are? Do you have a strong belief system? Can you create your character from the inside out by tapping the wealth of feelings, values, beliefs, perception your have residing inside?

There are talented writers who never reach their full potential because they are emotionally removed from their vast reservoir of resources and they try to manipulate their characters from the outside in order to maintain a safe distance from their feelings.

A prolific young screenwriter who attended one of my workshops always came up with terrific stories and characters, but his execution was always clichéd and boring. He would have creative meetings, take suggestions and make changes but he never seemed to improved his work and consequently never had success selling his scripts.

Finally, after a year of revisions I read his script and since his protagonist was passive and dull, it seemed obvious to me that he had the wrong person as the main character. I suggested he make another character, the brother, who was very active in the script, the main character. So he wrote from the brothers viewpoint. However, the new protagonist was just as dull and boring as the other had been before. The writer was so frustrated and upset, that I suggested he stop writing the script and work on something new, because he had been working on the same script for over a year and was really depressed.

He said, "I just can't give it up. I don't know why, but I just have to write this script."

Listening to his commitment, I realized there was more to this situation then writing the script and concluded it probably had to do with some "unfinished business" from his past. We met each week and he always came in with his script, but eventually he put the script aside and started to talk about himself and how much trouble he had with his past. One of his biggest problems was he couldn't remember his childhood and felt removed from his emotions, operating strictly on an intellectual level. After a few sessions it became clear the story he was writing was about his real brother and himself—a painful relationship that had ended in each being estranged from the other. They hadn't spoken in years and the situation was never resolved. When I probed into his feelings about the rift he replied, "It doesn't bother me at all." And dismissed the question.

I persisted, "If you have blocked your emotions and cut-off your feelings you won't be able to write with any emotional depth and you'll also never resolve your past hurts."

I gave him writing exercises and he eventually became aware of how much he missed his brother and began to deal with his disappointment and pain. During his journey beneath his mask he realized the main character, a policeman in the script, was in reality himself, and the other character, an alcoholic brother was a dark subpersonality of himself that he had disowned. As he reached into his feelings, he eventually let the tears begin to flow and as he did his emotional writing began to flow.

This was such a powerful insight for him, that it freed him and he no longer had to suffer over his writing, and finished his script in a couple of weeks.

As he began to integrate the different aspects of his personality he also began to write from his different characters and put those new feelings and emotions, that had been submerged, into his characters' voices to create emotionally diverse characters. His agent immediately sold his script to a major studio and he continues to be a prolific and successful, emotional writer.

Creating fictional characters who have similar problems to your own, often gives you the opportunity to work through a situation as on a trial basis or as a "dress rehearsal" for future actions you will take in your own life. It allows you to right the wrongs of your past. Through your characters your voice can speak and say all the things you're afraid to say in your own life. Writing is healing and I have often seen many writers get more therapeutic benefits through writing than through therapy!

By journeying beneath your persona or mask you'll be able to go beneath your character's masks to the real person inside. You can't explore your original voice until you allow that voice to speak from the inside out. Just for now, you're going to remove your mask and write from the person you were meant to be by finding your internal voice, the one buried behind your mask. This is really the only honest way to write.

When you connect to your feelings, emotions and dreams buried in your unconscious, magic happens in your writing. Your authentic voice enables you to move your audience, to get them to laugh, to cry and to feel. The truly great artists are those who are able to reveal their inner most voices in their writing.

Let your feelings emerge as you become a detective and discover the mysteries inside of you. Be a method writer and explore your deepest fears and give parts of yourself to your various characters. Begin your journey of self-exploration to re-acquaint yourself with all the characters inside. Dig out the ones who are hiding beneath layers of protective coverings, those lurking in the shadows and recesses. Reclaim these parts of yourself and give them to your fictional characters.

Allow your fictional characters to express what these internal voices, silent for years, need to say. Channel your voice and speak what you must speak through the voice of your characters. Writing from your inner cast of characters allows you to create dynamic, multifaceted characters, who are living and breathing human beings.

Expl,

To illustrate this point, I consulted with a talented writer who began working on a screenplay that was a thriller. Her major writing problem was the main character was weak and acted like a victim. I suggested she give her main character a stronger personality. No matter what writing exercises I gave her, the female lead remained weak and unexciting. She just didn't seem able to connect with the stronger aspect of her own personality.

Finally, I asked her if she had trouble expressing her own anger in her personal life. She confessed anger was one emotion that was impossible for her.

"I only seem to be able to write from the victim's voice. I was never allowed to get angry, as a child and I don't know how to let my characters be angry!"

We continued to work on her anger through free writing exercises which I assigned to her. By having her write about her childhood anger that she wasn't allowed to express, she recovered a *Recovering a repressed memory* repressed memory. It turned out her father physically abused her and she was shocked with the recovered memories. Of course, as a helpless child, she couldn't fight back, so she put her feelings underground and never emotionally experienced her anger or rage.

I told her to write about the first time he beat her when she was a small child, as she recalled how it happened. She was to visualize the scene and write in first person will all of her senses of touch, taste, sound, smell, and sight. Then I told her to rewrite the scene but this time she had to express her anger. The purpose of the exercise was to give her permission to feel angry and to fight back against her abuser; to say all the things she never was allowed to say.

Through the writing she was finally able to experience her anger. It took weeks of being unable to write the scene, until one day she came in with a powerfully dramatic scene, where she was not only able to express her anger, but also able to retaliate and get revenge. It was an explosive scene and in it she re-experienced her own pent-up anger and rage.

Through doing this exercise she finally was able to create a strong emotional character. By reconnecting to her repressed rage and pain, her writing took a qualitative leap to a much deeper level. From that point on her characters voiced their feelings and new characters emerged—a powerful, who had a strong voice able to express emotions. And the added benefit was that she started to express her anger in her own life as well. Her screenplay now had an active rather than passive main character, who no longer sounded like a victim.

It's important to call upon the different aspects of your own personality that you've probably ignored or have not expressed to create different aspects of your characters' personality. Remember, that you can't give to your characters those feelings and aspects of yourself which you can't give to yourself! YOU are all the characters.

Replace "will" with "through" or "with"

The following are seven steps to learn how to tap into your inner cast of characters and stories.

7 STEPS FOR WRITING FROM YOUR INNER SELF

- LISTEN TO YOUR INTUITION. Trust your "gut" feelings and instinct about your characters and stories.
- BE PASSIONATE ABOUT YOUR CHARACTERS. Know your characters inside out. Live with them, fight for them and nurture them.
- HAVE A VISION. Believe in your ideas! Feel strong about your values, beliefs and point-of-view.
- JOURNEY BENEATH YOUR MASK. Tap into your inner world. Trust your real "Self."
- DISCOVER NEW VOICES. Write from your inner cast of characters. Allow new voices inside to be heard.
- WRITE FROM YOUR HEART. Take your childhood stories and emotions and transform them into original, salable scripts.
- GIVE THE GIFT OF YOURSELF. You are unique and original. Reveal yourself and let the world know who you are!

You can write about many things you haven't experienced and still be truthful to the character. For example, I had a screenwriter come to see me because she was given an assignment to write a screenplay about a married couple.

She said, "Rachel, how can I do this assignment, I've never been married?"

I asked, "Are you writing a documentary about marriage, or are you writing about a man and a woman and their feelings toward each other?"

She said, "I'm writing about their relationship."

I then asked, "Have you ever been in love and dealt with relationship problems? Have you ever felt jealous, lack of trust, passion, insecurity, love, lust and hate?"

Of course her answer was yes, and she realized as we spoke that although she hadn't been married, she certainly had experienced the same emotions and feelings others in love have, whether married or not. The same is true when you're forced to write about a set of characters created by someone else, as in a sitcom or hour episodic drama.

To make your stories fresh and unique is to bring your own personal feelings and pieces of yourself into the characters. Do you have to be a murderer to write about one, or a prostitute to portray one? Of course you don't. What you do have to do is take your murderous feelings or your sexual ones and put them into your characters. <u>When I say write what you know, I don't want you to always take me literally.</u> What I do want you to do is get in touch with the various feelings you know and write about them, so your writing and characters will be compelling, complex, and credible!

Most screenwriters who have success, usually can access their various selves and put those parts into their stories and characters, regardless of whether or not they have actually experienced the same situation. From television movies to films they achieve emotional honesty and passion when they write, because they access their inner writer.

So if you're not a mother, father, murderer, preacher, cheerleader, beauty queen, lawyer, you can still write about these characters by going beneath your own mask and connecting with all the various human beings residing there.

ARCHETYPAL CHARACTERS

The following is a list of archetypal characters who Dr. C. G. Jung, the Swiss psychiatrist, referred to as universal because they have been portrayed in every culture down through the ages. These archetypes have been imprinted in everyone's Collective Unconscious, which goes back to primitive man, where all emotions and feelings are collected.

These Universal characters live inside you—all of them, with some parts being more dominant than others. Open yourself to all of them—the good and the bad. Some of the most popular ones have frequently appear in films, books and television movies.

YOUR INNER CAST OF CHARACTERS

CRITICAL PARENT—UNSUPPORTIVE, UNLOVING, JUDGMENTAL, RESTRICTIVE PARENT—DISTANT, COLD.

LITTLE PROFESSOR—CHILD WHO MAKES PARENTS PROUD BY BEING MATURE AND BRIGHT.

THE PERFECT CHILD—DOES EVERYTHING RIGHT. GOOD LITTLE GIRL, GOOD LITTLE BOY, OBEDIENT, DUTIFUL.

THE FEMME FATALE—SEXPOT, SIREN, FLIRT.

THE LADIES MAN—HUNK, MACHO, STUD, DON JUAN, BEAU BRUMMEL.

AMAZON WO/MAN—CAPABLE, INDEPENDENT, AGGRESSIVE, SELF-SUFFICIENT, INVINCIBLE.

WITCH/BITCH—AGGRESSIVE, COLD, BITCHY, MANIPULATIVE.

WALLFLOWER—SHY, QUIET, LOW SELF-ESTEEM, INSECURE.

DICTATOR—THE BOSS, ORDERS EVERYONE AROUND, NEVER IS PLEASED, DEMANDING, INSENSITIVE, RUTHLESS.

REBEL—NONCONFORMIST, STUBBORN, RULE-BREAKER, GOES AGAINST THE GRAIN.

BIG SHOT—WANTS THE BEST CAR, THE BEST TABLE IN A RESTAURANT, DEMANDING, BRAGGART, PICKS UP THE CHECK.

MADONNA—MOTHER FIGURE, CARETAKER, HOMEBODY, IDEALIZED WOMAN.

VICTIM—WAITS TO BE TAKEN CARE OF, WANTS TO BE RESCUED, RIGHTEOUS, SELF-PITYING, POOR ME, AIN'T IT AWFUL.

LITTLE PRINCE/SS—SPOILED, WANTS TO BE WAITED ON, DOTED UPON, EXPECTS OTHERS TO CATER TO HIM/HER.

CARETAKER—CHARITABLE, MRS. FIXIT, HELPS OTHERS ALL THE TIME, ATTENDS FUNERALS, VISITS HOSPITALS, TAKES CARE OF EVERYONE.

PEOPLE PLEASER—PLEASES PEOPLE ALL THE TIME, HAS NO NEEDS OF OWN, WANTS PEOPLE TO LIKE HER/HIM.

JOKER—PRANKSTER, PLAYS PRACTICAL JOKES, CUT-UP, GETS IN TROUBLE, MISCHIEVOUS, ATTENTION SEEKERS.

VILLAIN—ANGRY, MANIPULATOR, REVENGER, AVENGER, KILLER.

HERO/HEROINE—OVERCOMES STRUGGLES, THE DRAGON- SLAYER, DOES HEROIC DEEDS, SAVES THE DAY.

PERFECTIONIST—COMPULSIVE-OBSESSIVE, UP-TIGHT, DRIVEN.

WARRIOR—SAVES THE DAY, FIGHTS OFF THE ENEMY, SUPER-HERO.

RESCUER—TRIES TO MAKE LOST SOULS FIND THE RIGHT PATH, LIKES TO PLAY FLORENCE NIGHTINGALE, TAKES IN STRAY DOGS, CATS AND PEOPLE.

MARTYR—WHAT I COULD HAVE, SHOULD HAVE DONE, SELF-PITYING AND SELF-SACRIFICING AND LETS YOU KNOW IT.

CRITIC—BEATS YOU UP, NEEDLES YOU, JUDGMENTAL, NEGATIVE PROGRAMMING—CRITICAL VOICES FROM THE PAST, OWN WORSE ENEMY.

VULNERABLE LITTLE CHILD—HELPLESS, CRYING, HYPER- SENSITIVE, DEPENDENT.

SHADOW SELF—FILLED WITH LUST, GREED, RAGE, THE DARK SIDE, JEALOUSY, REVENGEFUL SELF YOU DON'T WANT TO ADMIT, MURDEROUS FEELINGS, DARK THOUGHTS.

THE WISE HIGHER SELF—CREATIVE, IMAGINATIVE, SPIRITUAL, LOFTY, INTUITIVE, INSTINCTUAL.

Embrace all of these interesting archetypal characters residing inside. Try to model your fictional characters after these different archetypes and your characters will be universal. Remember, powerful character development needs to come from inside so that your audience connects to them.

By learning how to write from your cast of characters you'll unlock the door to create unique and original characters, who touch the hearts of your audience. Call upon your inner cast of characters for they make-up the most unique, original and exciting character of all—YOU!

BLUEPRINT FOR SCREENWRITING

1. Write down all the characters living inside you. Read over your list and keep adding to your inner cast of characters.
2. Are you able to write with a strong voice? If the answer is no, why not?
3. Do you write from a victim's voice? Do all your characters sound like victims? If yes, write from a survivor's voice.
4. Write a scene from the opposite sex's point-of-view.
5. Do you acknowledge your shadow self, where you feel jealousy, envy, and rage? Write a scene from this inner character.
6. Are you frightened by your angry impulses and deny them? Write a scene and express your anger through a furious character.
7. How many masks do you wear? List them. Write a scene about the first time you put on your mask as a defense to protect you.
8. Follow the seven steps for writing from your inner self. 130

Chapter 15

Overcoming Writer's Block

"You get a writer's block by being aware that you're putting it out there."
—Frank Herbert

In one of my writing workshops a young man asked me, "Do you have to be psychotic to be a writer?"

At first, I thought he was kidding and waited for his laughter, but after a few moments of silence, I realized he was quite serious. I began to wonder how many other people believed the stereotype of the emotionally disturbed writer, holed up in his cold-water flat with a half empty bottle of vodka by his side, typing away in the wee hours of the morning.

Contrary to this romantic notion, a writer must have, at least, a semi-healthy ego and confidence in his or her work and him or herself. How else can one maintain any sort of belief in oneself when faced with constant rejection? How can the writer continuously motivate him or herself to write, if nothing he or she has written has been sold? How can one keep on writing when there's no positive reinforcement to spur one on? This is a pretty formidable task for even a very secure person to accomplish, let alone someone with a fragile ego.

Through the years I have counseled writers when they became blocked and have recognized different types of writer's block. This one-on-one counseling has provided me with tremendous insight into the myriad causes of writer's block. Some causes are obvious and others less so. Some writers successfully overcome their blocks, while others remain immobilized and unable to write. *SEPERATE THE*

Writing is about the most personal craft any artist can perform. It *WRITING* is always difficult for writers to separate the writing from them- *FROM YOUR* selves. If a writer is depressed, feeling blocked or angry, it is often re- *PERSONAL* flected in his writing. On the other hand, a musician can be angry *SELF* and still play his instrument, and a dancer can be depressed and still dance, without it affecting his art. *SOLUTIONS TO WRITING*

Many screenwriters become blocked almost daily when they first *BLOCKS* start to write, especially if they're writing a new scene. One good *1.* way to get unblocked when you start to write is not to start writing a new scene. Stop your work somewhere in the middle just before you end the scene you're working on during the previous day. The next time you start writing all you'll have to do is finish writing the scene you've been working on. This gets you started immediately before you worry about beginning a new scene.

The next time you're writing, rather then becoming blocked by having to switch gears with new material, you'll start writing imme- diately, because you'll know exactly where you're going and how to get there.

Another method you can use to prevent yourself from being *2.* blocked is actually rewriting a couple of pages you already have writ- ten, to get into the rhythm of your words. Your writing will just flow into the next scene.

I suggest to some writers who get blocked when facing the empty *3.* page to lightly put marks on the page with a pencil or pen, so they won't face the ominous blank page. It's a good idea to read your fa- *4.* vorite poetry for ten to fifteen minutes before you start to write. This gets your mind set into the meter and rhythm of the poem and al- lows you to become relaxed. It quiets your questioning mind. I have even suggested to writers who are uptight to meditate for five to ten *5.* minutes just before writing.

However these are rather basic techniques for overcoming writer's block, but writer's block can be a very complex phenomenon, and sometimes it's not that easy to break through, when you're blocked for deeper reasons.

When I consult with writers who are blocked I always find out what's going on in their life while they're working on their script. I do this so I can make a proper diagnosis, to determine whether the problem is with the WRITING or with the WRITER. I'm really serious. Sometimes writer's block has more to do with the writer and less to do with the writing.

There are writers who have been working on their screenplay literally for years, are so stuck and blocked they feel trapped and immobilized. Many times after talking to them, I find the problem has nothing to do with their writing, but has everything to do with what's going on in their life at present.

Because I strongly believe you can't separate the writer from the writing it's imperative to find out the root cause of the problem, before making recommendations on how to overcome the block.

Recently, an award-winning writer came to see me upon finishing her script, because she was blocked in her work and couldn't rewrite it.

She said, "I can't believe I wrote my screenplay without a main character! Every other character is interesting and exciting and my main character is inactive and boring. She's a victim. She isn't there. She's just an empty shell."

During our session as we discussed the script and why she was blocked, it soon became clear it was very autobiographical and I pointed out similarities between the main character and herself. She resisted my insight and became upset, because she didn't want to connect to that aspect of her personality, which she had disowned.

She kept feeling blocked and couldn't get a handle on the main character because she was too close to be objective. I tried to show her that her blind spot was exactly the same blind spot her heroine had which she was unable or unwilling to see the connection. Her main character's life mirrored her own life with the exact same issues. As we continued to work together on her current life problems she was resistant and still blocked. But soon we started to make some progress and she slowly worked on resolving her current problems. One day she blurted, "My God, I'm the main character!"

Finally, she was willing to look at herself and risk dealing with aspects of her life that were uncomfortable and hurtful, only after she admitted she was writing about her repressed self. By having the courage to realize the connection between herself and her main character, she overcame her block as she continued to solve her own personal problems. Of course, she then solved the main character's problems in her script and quickly rewrote it!

There are so many variables for writer's block. A writer's frame of mind is so important in relation to his work, that a simple solution to, "Why do I have writer's block," is never possible.

Recently, a writer who wanted advice on craft consulted with me because he was blocked and unable to finish the last part of his screenplay. He felt panicked since he was on a deadline with his producer. After I read his script I asked him, "Is there anything in the writing that's bringing up some unfinished business from your past?"

He talked about how he felt emotionally when he worked on his script. He told me about a particular painful childhood issue that kept surfacing during the writing. Together we discussed this "unfinished business," from his past and he was finally able to overcome his block and quickly finish his screenplay.

The block he had developed came from his own resistance to the material he was writing and the repressed feelings that arose during the writing process. To his credit he didn't give up, but kept working hard until he broke through the block.

The interesting point is this writer took his childhood material that originally caused him pain and transformed it into an arena of conflict between his characters. By writing from his childhood stories he was able to let go of the painful memories and work through his block. This fictional conflict turned out to be one of the high points of drama in his script. He wrote from his heart and created a dynamic script.

Another cause of writer's block happens because of the cruelty or insensitivity of other people. Several years ago, a young woman came up to me after a writing workshop and thanked me for helping her.

"I'm so grateful to you for making the workshop a safe place to read my work."

I asked her why.

She confessed, "I haven't written for over five years and this is the first time I was able to write anything. I had a writing teacher who tore my script apart in front of the entire class. I was so humiliated by his remarks. Maybe he didn't realize how he'd hurt me, but ever since then I lost all my confidence and haven't been able to write."

DESTRUCTIVE TEACHER

Few writers escape being blocked at some time during their writing career through taking workshops or being in writing groups. It's important for you not to let any teacher, colleague, friend, or family member be destructive in their criticism of your writing. Constructive criticism is fine, especially when someone makes a suggestion targeted to a specific writing problem. That is the only type of criticism I ever permit in my classes. Don't ever allow anyone to say, "You're writing stinks," "That isn't any good." "You can't write."

If you take a class and that happens with the teacher or with another student, run don't walk to the nearest exit and ask for your money back. On the other hand, writer's block might have nothing to do with thoughtless or insensitive criticisms, but can develop from the fragile balance the writer needs to have between maintaining motivation and enthusiasm in the face of self-doubt and self-criticism.

In my private therapy practice, I deal with many individuals concerning their personal relationships and inner conflicts. When they are relating their problems and recalling painful memories, many therapy clients experience a release from strong emotions they had suppressed for years.

After they dredge up these feelings in therapy and talk about them they often feel better and experience a lightness and a surge of new-found energy as they loosen the ties from the "ghosts of the past." They often have a sense of freedom and are better able to handle their present conflicts and relationships as they gain more insight.

writing as therapy

There are other individuals who have suppressed past experiences and continue suffering in the present. They can't seem to remember any details of their past and end up feeling blocked and frustrated. When this occurs I use writing exercises as a method to help them release the pent-up emotions they're unable or unwilling to verbalize. In these cases where the person is blocked, I discovered that writing, in place of talking, was a highly effective therapeutic and powerful tool to use with clients unable to recall their childhood. Through writing they were eventually able to release their block and discover their emotions.

The same phenomenon would also happen to certain writers in my workshops. When their script involved a personal story dealing with some painful aspect of their past, their repressed feelings would manifest themselves in writer's block. With my help and guidance the writers would work through their creative or psychological blocks. I would tell them to stop writing their script and start doing specific writing exercises. These exercises helped them work through their personal blocks. After doing the exercises they broke free from their blocks. The wonderful breakthroughs which they made in their writing allowed them to experience many of the same positive benefits clients experienced in therapy.

To further illustrate this point let me relate a few actual examples. I've changed the names of those students involved to protect their privacy.

A woman in one of my workshops, whom I'll call Nancy, was writing a script about a successful career woman and her teenage daughter. The mother was attractive whereas the daughter was plain and overweight. She was also unpopular in school and very unhappy with her mother. The two had a terrible relationship that kept getting worse. The daughter became more and more rebellious and the mother became more distant and involved in her work.

Nancy worked and worked on her story and couldn't figure out the ending. She kept going around in circles. First, she'd make the mother the main character. Then she'd rewrite the ending and change it so the daughter would be the main character. She couldn't get to the core of her story and kept going off on tangents. Her script had no focus, no resolution and it didn't work.

Every time a classmate would make a suggestion she would become angry and defensive. Rather then listen to the helpful criticism, she would argue and become upset. After a long struggle, Nancy finally set up the story so the two women would have a confrontation in the climax. The daughter would confess she was secretly jealous of her mother and the mother would break down and reveal that she'd always felt inadequate as a mother. She used her work as an escape from their relationship. In the end of the story the daughter and mother discovered they truly loved each other. The two arrived at a new understanding and positive relationship.

The mother was finally able to express her love for her daughter and the daughter developed a loving attitude toward her mother and in herself.

Nancy was like a new person after she finished her script. She lost her defensive attitude and was much happier. She later told the class that the characters were difficult for her to deal with because she discovered while writing the script they really were her own mother and herself.

When Nancy selected to write this story she wasn't consciously aware of this relationship, but only after she began to get involved with the characters and their problematic relationship did she realize they were really autobiographical. Through the process of writing the script, Nancy was able to let go of the deep feelings of anger she felt toward her own mother who was now deceased. She eventually arrived at a new self-awareness about her mother and herself. Nancy was finally able to forgive her mother and in the process forgive herself. She began to release negative feelings from the past and turned them into positive ones. Writing this script was very therapeutic for her and enabled her to begin the healing process.

From the above example, you can see the need to be careful not to choose a story that is too personal, because it often doesn't work out to be such a rewarding experience as Nancy's. In spite of her frustration she didn't give up and kept on writing until she got it right. No matter how frustrating the writing became or how many unpleasant feelings that she experienced while writing her script, she had the determination to complete it.

From my perspective as both a psychotherapist and writing teacher, I often make a diagnosis based on whether or not the block is one of craft or with the writer himself. There are many reasons people become blocked and all blocks can't be treated the same. Working with blocks is as individual as the individual writers.

There are personal blocks that affect your work—blocks emanating from problems such as drinking, addictions, divorce, financial pressures, family dysfunction and conflicted relationships.

Then there are blocks the result from working environments with pressured deadlines, worrying about results, stress, poor working conditions, job insecurity, ratings, negative environment, the bottom line and fear of only being as good as your last sale.

In other cases writers may use writer's block to focus all their energy on the writing and avoid dealing with other problems existing in their lives. Maybe they've had a bad personal relationship, suffer from depression or feel stuck in a "going nowhere" job. By developing writer's block and constantly obsessing over it, they can ignore what's really bothering them. The block can be a form of avoidance, protecting them from failure, pain and rejection. *[Writer's block as a shield or defense mechanism]*

Sometimes the reasons you may give for being blocked have nothing at all to do with writing. They are merely excuses to rationalize what you might be too afraid to do. These blocks often stem from an unconscious need for self-protection. How can you be rejected if you don't write? How can you get hurt if you're not criticized? How can you be a failure if you can't produce? *[Fears]*

Fear is all encompassing when you are a writer. There are often psychological causes for blocks, that emerge from your internal forces such as insecurity, fear of failure, fear of success, fear of rejection, negative self-talk, unrealistic expectations, procrastination, depression and repressed emotions. These are all defenses formed to protect you against fear.

But let's suppose you aren't developing writer's block as a defense mechanism. Let's say you desperately want to write more than anything in the world. You sit at your typewriter or computer day after day and you can't write. You feel frustrated, depressed and life is unbearable, because you can't do the thing you love to do most—WRITE. You stare at the blank page and panic. Where to start? What to write? A small voice whispers in your ear, "You don't have anything exciting to say." *[Negative self-talk or inner critic]*

The voice gets louder as it laughs, "Look who's trying to write. You know it'll be rejected!" Soon the laughter drowns out your thoughts and ideas and you aren't able to produce any words onto the empty page. Every day you go to your computer to write and the well is dry. If this is the case you are truly blocked!

I have identified the following six stumbling blocks that prevent writer's from having success with their writing. All of these blocks are different aspects of FEAR!

6 STUMBLING BLOCKS TO WRITING

1. Procrastination
2. Fear of success/failure
3. Fear of rejection
4. Psychological and creative blocks
5. Inner critic
6. Negative frame of mind

These culprits are responsible for most of the problems you experience when you sit down to write and become immobilized. They are responsible for preventing you from getting started, from finishing projects, keeping you stuck in the middle of your work. These stumbling blocks create resistance to writing itself. They diminish belief in ones' talent and ability, preventing you from getting your work into the marketplace. They also can cause low self-esteem and insecurity, decreasing creativity, while increasing stress and depression.

What happens when you become blocked? Do you give up in frustration? Do you obsess over your block? Next to each block write about how each affects you? From which of these do you suffer the most? All of them? None of them? Some of them? Identifying your block is the first step to overcoming it.

The following exercise will enable you to identify and overcome your specific block. Read over the six stumbling blocks. Now rate each block from 1–6, the worst block being number 1. After you've written how these symptoms block you, you are on the path toward overcoming them, because you are now aware of what specific blocks you have. This awareness is the first step to overcoming a problem. The second step is writing anyway. Just write in spite of being blocked. Just take the action and write.

Although these states can cause writer's block, the two most prevalent are procrastination and the inner critic. They are the two biggest stumbling blocks to writing success. The most common reasons for procrastination are usually psychological and unconscious—hidden from your awareness. On the one hand if you desperately want to write and yet don't, this can cause you great pain and suffering.

On what seems a conscious level you aren't willing to put in the hard work and discipline to overcome your blocks. However this is

Procrastination

really an internal conflict which may stem from fear of failure or fear of success. These fears will unconsciously sabotage any long term attempt to keep working on a script. They manifest themselves in the form of procrastination. They not only prevent you from completing your writing but eventually lead you to feelings of low self-esteem, guilt and shame.

Your internal messages may say to you, "Why don't you have any discipline or will-power?" "Why can't you set goals and reach them?" The questions remain unanswered, because the real reasons are safely hidden away in your unconscious, just waiting to attack you when you least expect. *Childhood influences.*

These fears are probably related to your childhood perhaps when a parent or teacher said, "That's not the way to do it," or "Can't you ever get anything right?" "Why can't you be perfect?"

Although these messages are different from fear of success, they all stem from the same source. The inner dialogue says, "You don't deserve to be successful." or "You aren't good enough to make it." In either case the outcome is the same—you procrastinate and don't write your screenplay. *Low Frustration tolerance*

Another reason you might procrastinate is you have what is called low frustration tolerance. This means you can never deal with frustrating situations or tasks, so you look for ways to avoid taking the action, which in this case means avoid writing. You might divert yourself with activities that provide immediate gratification and escape like eating, drinking, going to movies, talking on the phone, watching television, or even cleaning the refrigerator.

These activities take no discipline or concentration and relieve your inner anxiety. You then don't have to put in the long hours and master the craft of writing. You are blocked. *TAKE ACTION NOW*

One of the best ways to overcome procrastination is to enter therapy and explore your memories, dreams and unconscious and bring these negative messages into your awareness. However, a more direct way to overcome procrastination is through your behavior. TAKE ACTION! When you act against your fears you start to conquer them. Don't think about writing. Don't fantasize about writing. Don't worry about it or feel guilty about it. Just do it. Suddenly, you'll find the time and energy you wasted in procrastinating, you'll now use to get your writing completed.

Imagine if you will, that you are about to sit down and write when suddenly you're stopped in your tracks. The voice of your INNER CRITIC is beckoning you. When this happens you feel frustrated, lonely, angry, depressed, hopeless, and helpless. You ask yourself if you'll ever write again. You feel out of control and don't know where to turn. But all is not lost. Let's look at some steps you can take to deal with your inner critic and start writing again.

1.   The first thing you want to do is identify the inner voice who talks to you all the time. This voice that's filled with criticism, self-doubt and negativity. This is the voice whispering from your childhood and may be the voice of your critical parent, your peers, or your teachers. It's a voice that once belonged to someone from your past that you have now integrated as your own critical voice. It stops you before you even get started writing. It fills you with insecurity and doubt about your ability to write. It damages your self-esteem and blocks your creativity.

What can you do about it? How can you get rid of it? One of the successful techniques I have developed is the following exercise.

2.   Write down all the negative self-talk you hear every time you start to write. Why don't you do that right now. When you hear the critical voice immediately write down whatever it's saying to you. It could say things like: "Get a real job." "Look who's trying to be a writer." "You have nothing new to say." "There are too many good screenplays already written." "Get serious! You can't write."

These are a few examples of the put downs you say to yourself, before you even get started to write. All these negative messages and self-talk makes it almost impossible to write. They stop you in your tracks before you even get started. You have to know how you're stopping yourself by jotting down your negative self-talk as fast as you can as you're experiencing it. Read over everything you've written. Is all of it true? Part of it? None of it?

Fill the entire page. The next step is to recognize whose voice is talking to you. You'll break through your block by identifying the voice! Whose voice is it—mother's, father's, relatives, peers, teacher's? Or is the voice a combination of all of them?

After you've identified the person or persons shouting all these insults at you, write down their name next to each negative remark. Read over the criticisms once again. Now ask yourself if

what they're saying about you is true. Next, take a clean sheet of *3.*
paper and write a dialogue with the person(s) who said all those
horrible things about you and your writing ability. Tell them all the
things you wanted to say, but never was allowed to express. It
would have been too scary for you and you would've probably been
punished.

Let them know how you feel about what they've said to you and
how it hurt you all these years. After you've written to them you'll
probably realize how silly and ridiculous it is for you to allow people
from your past to still have this power over you. Don't permit their
criticisms to stop you in your tracks when you want to write and realize the voice is not telling you the truth. So take away it's power to
block you. Stop listening and start writing.

Carry a notebook and record your negative self-talk every time *4.*
you hear it. (I imagine you'll be writing most of the day at first.) By
writing the criticisms down you will see how insidious your negative
self-talk is and what a hold it has on your writing ability and on your
self-esteem.

Continue to write positive statements beside the negative remarks to counteract them. You've been carrying around this critical
voice for years. Now is the time to let go of your inner critic and silence it by refuting what it says. Take away its power and give your
creativity back to yourself.

Now, create a written list of positive statements about yourself as *5.*
a writer and read them over until you memorize them. Use these to
silence your inner critic as soon as it begins to criticize you. Remember the inner critic has had a full time job criticizing your writing and
you, so you must be vigilant in your counterattack. Next time the
"inner critic" starts shouting negative comments to you—IGNORE
IT! Tell it to be quiet.

For 21 days read your positive statements every morning when *6.*
you wake up and every evening before going to bed. Believe what
you've written. If you don't believe in yourself and take yourself seriously as a writer who will? These techniques really work and writers have overcome blocks by diligently working hard to break
through them.

Breaking free from blocks can be an exciting, exhilarating, experience! When you overcome your writer's block a wonderful thing

happens—you'll feel a new sense of "lightness" and freedom when you write. To this end I have developed ten keys for you to unlock your blocks.

BLUEPRINT FOR SCREENWRITING

10 KEYS TO UNLOCK YOUR BLOCKS

1. STAY IN THE MOMENT.
2. SUSPEND CRITICAL JUDGMENTS.
3. BE OPEN TO ALL POSSIBILITIES.
4. FORGET ABOUT RESULTS.
5. SILENCE YOUR "INNER CRITIC."
6. BE IN THE PROCESS AND NOT THE PRODUCT.
7. EMBRACE YOUR PLAYFUL CHILD.
8. LOSE YOUR "SELF."
9. BE COURAGEOUS.
10. REVEAL YOURSELF.

Writer's block is really pent-up creative energy. When you break free from your block a tremendous amount of this stored up creativity and energy will come bursting forth. Overcoming blocks gives you freedom to make your writing a joyful experience, where you are having fun with words, excitement with your ideas and pleasure in the writing process!

Chapter 16

The Completed Screenplay

"I usually have a sense of clinical fatigue after finishing a book."
—John Cheever

You have followed your Blueprint for Screenwriting and by now have constructed your finished product—your screenplay. It's your calling card that shows you can write a properly structured, solid story and develop complex, interesting characters.

Given all the harsh realities about writing and having completed your Blueprint For Screenwriting, do you still want to be a writer? Have your motives for becoming a writer changed after all the time, effort and hard work you've put into completing your writing project?

Do you still want success? Do you still want to be rich and famous? Or must you write your beliefs, hopes and burning desires and share your vision with the world? If the answer to the last question is "yes," then you must continue with your writing and don't stop until you reach your goals.

I've developed a checklist for you, to be your blueprint when you're developing a new script. It shows all the necessary elements

150

to include, and the proper building blocks to use for great structure. Here are the guidelines for you to follow and keep this check list near you to refer to when you're creating your blueprint for screenwriting. And you'll always be heading in the right direction— writing a successful screenplay.

BLUEPRINT FOR SCREENWRITING—
CHECKLIST FOR SUCCESS

1. Do you have only one main character?
2. Does your main character have a desperate goal he wants to reach?
3. Do you know your ending first and then work backwards to the beginning?
4. Does your opening set off the action of the story?
5. Is your main character active and not passive?
6. Do you have conflict in every scene?
7. Does every character in your work move the main character's story forward?
8. Do you hook your audience and reader by the first 10 pages?
9. Does every scene relate to your plot structure or spine?
10. Does your work have a single storyline?
11. Are all of your scenes written in a cause-and-effect manner? How do you know this?
12. Is there an emotional relationship between your main character and another character? If yes, with whom?
13. Does your main character change in the climax?
14. Is your plot resolved in the climax?
15. Does each scene have a single purpose? Write it in a sentence or two.

* You know this because if you remove one scene, the story falls apart.

Afterword:
How to Survive
the Writing Game

"Henceforth I ask not good fortune. I myself am good fortune."
—Walt Whitman

For those of you who have completed your screenplay and want to pursue selling it, the following information is for you. I have written this to make your journey a realistic one. And also to give you some valuable tips to help you stay on the right career track.

At the Writer's Center, I teach writers techniques for developing a writer's survival kit which includes, career strategies, communication skills, how to present yourself, how to network, how to get recognition, and how to get people to listen to your ideas. These writers are often amazed at how little they know about the business aspect of the writing business. Because most writers have to sell themselves, as well as their writing, they are at a definite advantage over the competition, if they know techniques to help them succeed in the writing game.

In the new millennium it's more difficult than ever to be a screen-writer because of all the competition and diminishing sources. Doing business is tough and only the competitive and resourceful writers will survive. Production companies, networks and movie studios are now divisions of conglomerates, where more executives are interested in the bottom line rather than in the creative line.

BOTTOM LINE

Even if it isn't bought by a network or studio to be made into a film, don't despair. Many writers have gotten assignments to write other projects after executives have read their screenplays and were impressed with the writer's writing ability. No one will hire you if you don't have a sample of your writing to show. All the people involved in the financial end of a project must be assured you know how to start, structure, and complete your work. They only get this assurance by seeing your ability to lay out the story's structure, create exciting characters, motivate them, write fresh dialogue and have a working knowledge of plotting a story from the beginning to the climax.

OVERVIEW

Once in a while, you might be lucky enough to get a director, producer or star interested in your script. If they like it, they could take it to the networks as a package deal. This means your screenplay would have a major star or director or production company attached as part of a package, and makes it more attractive to those in charge. This is especially true if the star, producer or director involved has a lot of commercial popularity.

Package deal.

When you enter the world of business—and this is the writing business—it's always good to have some hard evidence of who you sent your project to and when you sent it. So begin to keep records of each submission, who you submitted it to and the date. This is in case your work gets lost and also to give you a time-frame for making a follow-up call to see the status of your work.

SUBMISSION DATA

In the worse case scenario your correspondence could serve as a paper trail, if you ever felt your work was plagiarized or used without your permission. In no other business does an individual have to put him or herself on the line more than a writer. Every time he or she pitches an idea, writes a screenplay, produces a project, sends a query letter or meets with a producer, he or she's in a vulnerable position. And nobody is less qualified to do business than writers. Why? Because writers spend most of their time mastering their craft and none of their time learning how to sell.

PAPER TRAIL

WHY WRITERS ARE UNPREPARED TO DO BUSINESS.

You study, go to workshops, perfect your craft and when you finally write your greatest screenplay to the best of your ability, pouring your heart and soul into the writing, you're completely unprepared for the next step of the writing game: You have to market yourself in an over-crowded marketplace, where the supply of talent greatly exceeds the demand. You soon discover paying one's dues isn't enough and that you have to deal with people who make decisions about your writing and future, not based on the merit of the writing itself, but on many other variables. Yet, a single "yea" or "nay" can break a career or break a heart.

Over the past decade of witnessing the devastating effects of this business, I realized there were few resources available for those who must constantly go into the marketplace, unprepared both in the business techniques and marketing skills it takes to sell their writing. And the fall-out of this constant "putting oneself on the line" creates self-doubt and low self-esteem.

There is a plethora of writers who have written wonderful books, scripts and screenplays who have felt that completing the writing was enough. But in truth it's the ability to market and sell their writing that allows them to survive the writing game. Producing a portfolio of your scripts is great, but it's only the first step.

You have to have a plan and a blueprint for selling your screenplay. You want to learn who the decision makers are and how to reach them, rather than dealing with entry-level employees in the organizations. Many beginning writers think all they have to do is finish writing and it will be sold. Some never realize the writing process is really comprised of not only writing the script but includes selling the script, if that's your goal.

You have to be adept in both areas to be successful and to become a person who can convince other people what a terrific writer you are. You have to sell agents, producers, managers, network executives on your idea and on you. You hate to sell? Well, wait a minute—you're selling all the time, wherever you go, whoever you meet, whatever you say. Remember, you are always selling yourself, whether you're conscious about doing so or not.

What do you say about yourself before you say anything? What self-image do you want to create when you go about selling your script? Become aware of your clothing, your posture, your facial expression, your gestures, your hair, your eye contact, your handshake. You can plan in advance what image you wish to project. Projecting a positive self-image will help to sell your screenplay. Your script can be the most wonderful masterpiece in the world, but if you present a negative self-image as a writer you won't sell anything. You don't get a second chance to make a first impression. Make yours an unforgettable one.

SPEAKING YOUR PITCH

I have worked with many talented writers who never were able to sell their writing. Not because they didn't know how to write, but because they didn't know how to speak! You have to make it easy for people to want to listen to you. Preparation is the answer to getting *1* listened to. Do you have enthusiasm in your voice, are you excited *2* about what you're saying? Are you credible in what you say and how *3* you say it? Do you speak in a monotone, in a whisper, so fast nobody can understand you?

4 When you present your idea don't apologize, hesitate, become *5* embarrassed. Speak in a strong voice, using direct eye contact and *6* emote in a clear and confident manner. When you have to talk to an agent or producer on the telephone, it's often good to write out the script of what you want to say and practice it until you can speak like you believe what you're saying.

7 Have you mastered your three-sentence pitch? What is your first sentence, your second sentence, your third? Write the sentences *8* down and study your pitch. Have you grabbed your listener's interest and attention? Does it sound interesting and focused?

9 Practice your pitch into a tape recorder before you have a meeting. Anticipate any questions or objections in advance, so you can *10* have prepared answers. Think of what kind of resistance you might encounter when you present your work and figure out how *11* to overcome the resistance of others without becoming defensive. *12* Remember, you're a professional writer and you need to create the image of one.

13 When you're pitching your script and an executive makes suggestions or starts changing the focus of your screenplay—let them! You want to get the person you're pitching to, excited and involved *Don't say this* in your script. So let them give you any suggestions, listen to their ideas and keep quiet when they talk. Don't say, "I don't like your suggestions," or "That's not what I meant."

People in decision-making positions, like to think their ideas *14*
are great, so don't tell them anything different until they're sold
on your script! Unfortunately, I have seen many mediocre writers
sell their screenplays, while more talented writers don't. This is
unfair, but so is life. Many writers have sold merely on the merits */5*
of their self-presentation and their ability to sell and not on their
ability to write.

Self-esteem is the key to success or failure in anything you do. So *Self-*
many writers suffer from feelings of inadequacy and believing that *esteem*
they aren't enough, especially when it comes to selling themselves.
Self-esteem is based on what you think and feel about yourself and
not what someone else thinks and feels about you! You must have
self-esteem, not only to keep you motivated when you're writing,
but especially when you start selling your screenplay. If you don't,
the first rejection will put you into a tailspin and you'll come crashing down to the lower depths.

When you submit your writing you first need a plan. Do your re- *TARGET*
search into the companies you want to send your script to. If you've *your*
written a science fiction script and the production company or *SCRIPT*
movie studio makes nothing but action adventures, forget it, you *TO THE*
don't stand a chance. If you've written a romantic comedy, don't *RIGHT*
send your script to a producer who only makes horror films. Study *STUDIO,*
the market before you make your submissions. Target your script to *ETC,*
the right studio, network or production company.

If you get a rejection, don't take it personally! The last thing you *DON'T*
should do is base your self-esteem with getting rejected or accepted. *TAKE*
All this means is your product is not what the company is buying. *REJECTION*
Just look at it as you're not selling what they want to buy. File the re- *PERSONALLY*
jection away, while you put another script into the mail. Many successful screenwriters never sold their first script until after they sold
their second or third scripts. *WHAT TO DO WHILE WAITING*

Don't sit around and wait for the phone to ring or the mail to *FOR A*
come. Keep busy! Have interests and a life outside of writing. Live *REPLY*
your life as fully as you can while waiting for an answer. The best
thing to do is start another project and keep writing during this waiting period. Besides, you do need a body of work and now is the time
to be productive. If you can afford it now would be a good time to get
away and germinate some new ideas for your next script. Nothing is

better for your creative spirit then to be relaxed, unstressed and out of the pressure cooker. So go get some needed R & R.

VIEW YOUR SCRIPT AS A PRODUCT TO SELL

In some of the previous chapters I stressed the importance to write from your heart and write from your life experiences. Now, that you're wanting to sell your screenplay you must do the opposite. Now, is the time to emotionally remove yourself and your personal attachment to the writing and treat it as a product you're trying to sell. I know this is easier said than done, but it's necessary. Look at your screenplay with an objective writer's eye and remove yourself emotionally from the writing. Sure you're going to feel depressed if you're rejected, but you can't let it get you down.

Your motivation to sell your script must be internal and come from you. Your desire to produce and sell your writing must be your goal and not one you're wanting for someone else. Your writing ability can't be dependent on whether someone in BCA Company rejected your script or not.

FOLLOW UP CALL

Always have your script out there. Continue to send it out no matter what happens. If you haven't heard after a reasonable amount of time, follow up with a phone call or a personal letter. Many times I have had to call or write a letter to find out the status of my script after I had sent it out to production companies, studios and agents.

Your script is not the only one they are concerned about, but it certainly is the only one you're interested in. It's up to you to follow up if you don't know what's the status. Even if your writing is rejected by everyone you've sent it to, find more places to send it to. Failure is not in being rejected. Failure is giving up trying. And who's to say that your next submission won't be the one that's bought!

In the writing game, you must have an unswerving belief in yourself and in your work. On the other hand you also must be flexible enough to make changes in your script when they're warranted. Don't wear blinders and let your ego take over your better judgment. If you hear the same criticism over and over again listen to it and do the necessary rewriting. If you're not certain what to do, consult with a script consultant like myself or others. When you feel your screenplay is absolutely the best it will ever be, then is the time to stick to your guns and be firm.

SCRIPT CONSULTANT

I remember when I wrote my first non-fiction book and I got a call from an agent in New York who wanted to represent me. She started telling me what changes she wanted me to make in the manuscript. Because she was my first agent, I was ready to rewrite the entire book. Lucky for me, I spoke with an experienced writer who told me, "Don't make any changes for this agent, until she finds a publisher who wants you to sign a contract, then tell her you'll be happy to make any changes they want."

OR

At first I was afraid to take her advice, but I eventually did. And you know what, the agent took me on as a client without my changing a single word. On the other hand, I have also made changes when I felt an agent's or producer's notes were absolutely right. So use your intuition, your good judgment and your faith in yourself and let your common sense tell you what to do when the situation presents itself.

And above all, don't lose confidence or belief in yourself and your writing, especially if you feel you've given it your all. Look at the criticism not from your ego but with a professional writer's eyes and objectivity. Be professional enough to let go of things that don't work and change your material even if it means rewriting the entire script. But remember at some point you must believe in your work, no matter what! If you don't, you'll constantly be affected by every rejection, until you'll find yourself unable to write. *BE FLEXIBLE BUT WITH CONVICTION*

The writing game is difficult enough to play and if you want to win, don't sabotage yourself. In other words "Don't stab yourself in the back." Take good care of yourself, eat properly, exercise, have friends and interests and have a life besides writing. *KEEP BALANCED*

Take a course in marketing or selling. If you get too depressed and it affects your entire life when your script gets rejected, seek help from a professional therapist. In any situation where you are the creator of your product it is very difficult to sustain your motivation, if you're always feeling depressed and hopeless. *TAKE A SELLING OR MARKETING COURSE* *GET HELP FOR DEPRESSION*

Wishing, hoping, praying or just working hard isn't enough to gain you the professional recognition you want. First you must decide what you want to write and then target the studios or networks. Next, create a plan to reach your goals, whatever they are. Don't wait for others to do it for you and that includes even those of you who have an agent. It's ultimately up to you to get what you want for yourself. *STEPS 1. 2.*

3.   How can you sell me on you and your writing abilities, if you're embarrassed to tell me all the good things about yourself? Create a "brag sheet" listing all your attributes as a writer and as a person. List everything you've written, your credits, your resume—all the projects you want to write. Read your brag sheet over every day and every night, until you start believing you have credibility.

     Do you hear an inner voice saying, "It's not nice to brag." Well, don't listen to that voice anymore! And what's the matter with saying good things about yourself to other people. You sure don't have a problem saying negative things, do you?

     People believe what you say about yourself, so start listening to all of the negative things you tell everyone. Change the things you say to positives. Just for practice, team up with another writer and spend five minutes telling him what a terrific writer you are and how excited you are about your latest writing project. How did you do? That wasn't too hard was it? How did you feel saying nice things about yourself? My guess is it wasn't easy for you to do.

     But practice makes perfect. Ask your friend to give you honest feedback on how convincing you sounded. Work on improving those things you need to improve. Practice makes perfect and that goes for saying good things about yourself. So get in the practice of answering with a positive response when someone says, "Hi, how are you doing?"

     "Great, I'm so excited about the script I just finished. I can't wait to get it out there."

     This will create a positive reaction in other people about you and your work and the next time they see you they'll remember that you're doing good work. People want to associate with winners, not losers. And in the writing game, you certainly want to present yourself as a winner, even if you've never sold anything. How can anyone have the confidence to put large sums of money into your project if you don't believe in it? They can't. So it's time to now start creating a winning image of yourself as a writer.

     This leads me to one of the most pervasive problems writers have. Answer this question. "Do you take yourself seriously as a writer?" Think about it before you answer. Are you able to introduce yourself as a writer? If you aren't, why not? Are you able to think of yourself as a writer? If not, why?

How to Create a Winning Attitude Towards Writing, Submitting, and Rejection. [handwritten annotation]

Your winning attitude all begins with you. Now is the time for you to take yourself seriously as a writer! Once again, if you don't, I certainly won't and neither will the agents or producers, or network and studio executives to whom you're trying to sell your script.

Successful writers don't live in fear and aren't afraid of making mistakes and taking risks after their work is rejected. When their writing is rejected they still stay committed to their writing until they find people who will like their work. They remain passionate about their writing and don't give up. Why is it we always put ourselves down for being rejected by our negative self-talk, instead of praising ourselves after taking a risk over and over and over again, by constantly and consistently sending our work out. Just think how you would treat another writer if he or she got rejected. Would you tell him or her something along the lines of:

"Don't put yourself down." "It's the work that got rejected, not you." "Dr. Seuss was rejected over 56 times before his first book was published." "They don't know good writing when they see it." *Dr Seuss rejected 56x.* [handwritten annotation]

But is this what you say to yourself? I'm sure that you aren't that kind or gentle to yourself. Well, now is the time to nurture yourself just like you nurture other people. You need to recognize how much negative programming you have and deliberately counteract it when you are rejected. Write down positive affirmations about yourself and your work and read them over, especially when you get rejected. *Maintaining Motivation* [handwritten annotation]

As I said earlier, your motivation for continuing to write can't come from other people, it must come from inside you. Now is the time to get back to your reasons for wanting to be a writer in the first place and don't let anyone or any outside circumstances take you away from your goal. Without that internal belief and trust in yourself and your work, you'll never make it as a writer. You must continue to send your product out week after week without giving up or getting down. *Meet Other Writers* [handwritten annotation]

Everyone gets rejected and having a community of writers to talk to and pour your heart out to is essential. Find other writers to meet with and develop a support system or network of writers, especially when dealing with marketing and rejection. Writers need all the support they can get and in my Writer's Support Groups we give emotional support, career support, and craft support. We deal with writers' personal and professional issues such as writer's block, dealing with rejection, overcoming procrastination.

I coach writers on how to play the writing game, giving them techniques and strategies on how to speak and act on interviews, at pitch meetings, and on the telephone. These skills are especially important for those writers who work in the entertainment industry and constantly have to pitch their ideas. There is no other industry which is as dysfunctional as the entertainment industry. I've seen talented writers with fabulous scripts get rejected and writers who couldn't write be given hundreds of thousands of dollars for their script, then have the studios hire other writers to write it.

Breaking the rules

By now you have learned how to successfully play the writing game by the rules. And speaking of rules, I have found that sometimes ignorance is bliss. For example, a couple of years ago, two writers from another state, came to Los Angeles to consult with me on their script. They came a day early so they could visit agents and since they didn't know the rules, they found the addresses of the agents who they wanted to represent them. They didn't call but went directly to their offices and said they wanted to meet with the agent. And do you know what? They got one. Of course, it was on the merits of their script, but on the other hand, if they knew the rules they would have NEVER barged into agents offices without an appointment or a personal referral.

So after you know the rules, you sometimes need to break them. What better way to get an appointment or meeting with a producer, an agent or a studio executive, then to be creatively outrageous or unique in your approach. Let your imagination soar and find original ways to become visible.

Don't listen to bad advise

In the writing game, criticism seems to be easier to give than praise and everyone is a Monday morning quarter-back. People in the entertainment industry are constantly telling writers what's not working in their script. The balance between criticism and writing is difficult for many to maintain. This is because you're allowing yourself to be affected by the whims and wiles of other people, who often make their decisions, not on the merits of your script, but on their own subjectivity, their own ego needs, and their own insecurities.

Unfortunately, some people who give advice (solicited or not) and who are in the position to okay a project often have little or no knowledge of craft. In fact some people keep their jobs, especially in the entertainment industry by always saying "no," since it seems to be safer than putting oneself on the line and having the script turn on to be a flop or a financial disaster like *Howard the Duck*.

IT'S SAFER TO SAY "NO"

Recently, a writer asked me what he should do with his agent from a reputable agency, who liked a screenplay he wrote and decided to represent him. But his calls weren't returned, and the agent's secretary always had excuses for her boss (he was on the phone, in a meeting, out to lunch, out of town, out of the office, etc.). He asked for his script back and after having it one year, he discovered the agent only sent it out to five production companies.

Expl poor AGENT

"I was so frustrated, when I discovered it was only sent to five people in a year," he said. "Now, I have to start the process of getting an agent, all over again."

Like this young man, many people don't know what to expect from their agent, since most are just thrilled to get one in the first place. As in any business, you have to know the individual your dealing with and in the writing business, you have to learn what works best with your particular agent and what doesn't. Did you notice I used the word "business?" That's because getting an agent and dealing with one is a business and it's important for you to approach it as such. *DEVELOP A RAPPORT WITH YOUR AGENT*

Try to form a partnership with your agent and to develop a rapport. Get to know your agent's taste, so he or she will be excited with your work, because if your agent doesn't believe in your script, chances are it won't be sold.

Although it's difficult to get an agent, in truth, after you sign the contract, an agent works for you and is your employee. Sound strange? You probably can't even think in those terms, for in reality, you, like other writers, are thrilled to get an agent. It all goes back to the law of supply and demand and in this business, the demand for agents far exceeds the supply. *STRATEGIZE WITH YOUR AGENT*

Let me tell you a few strategies I suggested to writers in dealing with their agents. First, rather than being afraid to call or just sitting back and waiting for something to happen, we worked out a specific plan for them to be active in their own career. Rather than calling with a "I hope I'm not being a pest," attitude or "Have you heard from anyone, yet?" they called with specific information to help their agent like, "I ran into Bob Jones over at the studio and he'd like you to send over my script."

This change of attitude helped them form a better relationship with their agent. The writers began to feel more in control of their career and the agent began to have more respect for them. Recently, I invited an agent to speak at the Writer's Center. She made some wonderful points that I would like to share with you.

She told the group she had only so much time during the course of the day, and had to spread it out among a lot of writers. She asked the following question: "If I work with over fifty clients, and I'm try-ing to sell each one's work in only so much time, the question is:

'Who do you think your career is more important to—you or me?'

2. Do you get the message? It's up to you to do as much work as you can, to help your agent sell you and your writing. That means you must be active in trying to meet people in the business, you need to network (whether you like to or not) and you need to tell people what a terrific writer you are. You never know if the person next to you in line at the bank, couldn't be someone looking for a script!

3. This agent went on to say she likes a client who is prolific and keeps writing new projects no matter what! If your last screenplay was rejected, don't give up, but keep on creating new product. Most agents like clients who bring them new sample screenplays or televi-sion movies. They don't want you to just sit back and wait for that one script to sell. Agents want clients to have a body of work in which to show off their talent and the more product they have to sell the easier their job.

4. If you feel your relationship with your agent is like a bad marriage, get out. Don't waste your time and energy trying to make it better, because it probably won't be. Lastly, agents like to deal with writers

5. who are enthusiastic and confident about themselves and their work. It makes the selling of both, much easier, when a client can be personable and successfully handle a pitch meeting after the agent sets one up.

6. As in any relationship, you must have give and take and most of all mutual respect. This means you should be able to sit down with your agent and help in planning strategies to sell your work and to

further your writing career. Your relationship with your agent should be a partnership, with both of you having the same goal—your writing success.

By taking an active part in your career, being responsible for making new contacts, developing new writing products, and believing in yourself and your writing, you will help your agent achieve success for you and your career. You will than be a major player who will win the writing game!

So stick with your game plan and do the best writing you know how, have your personal vision and truth, and reach inside to put yourself into your script. One day someone will recognize your ability and talent, but in the meantime you need to keep writing, keep sending your work out and keep your writing goals in mind. You'll win the writing game if you're willing to improve your skills and master your craft, learn how to market yourself from the inside out, and above all be persistent. Just keep on writing no matter what and you'll not only survive, but you'll thrive in playing the writing game.

BLUEPRINT FOR WRITING

Here are 25 KEY questions you need to answer to create your blueprint for success to market yourself and your script.

1. Why aren't good screenplays enough?
2. What's the worst part about getting rejected?
3. Why do you need a market approach to your writing?
4. What are you selling? Who are you selling to?
5. What does your product look like?
6. What does your format look like?
7. What market are you selling to? What do they need?
8. Does your writing fit their needs?
9. What do you say about yourself before you say anything?
10. Write how others would describe you.
11. Write about what you want them to say.
12. What happens when you open your mouth?
13. How do you introduce yourself?
14. How do you talk about your writing?
15. Create a Brag Sheet. List all your credits, your writing ability, your talent.
16. List reasons why you take yourself seriously as a writer.
17. Introduce yourself as a writer.
18. Tell another person about your script.
19. List everyone you've ever met who could help you in the writing game.
20. List five ways you can make more contacts.
21. What do you do if you don't have an agent?
22. How do you get an agent?
23. What do you do after your work's rejected?
24. What are some of the personal barriers that might hold you back?
25. Develop a workable plan to survive the writing game.

Index

A

Acts, 83–86, 91–92
Antagonist, 53–54
Archetypal characters, 132–134

C

Causal writing, 36–37, 82–83, 91
Characters, 1, 20–21, 51–53, 109–110,
    see also Protagonist
  biography, 41–43
  conflict, 49–51, 81–82
  emotional arc, 58–61, 62–65,
    111–112
  from your inner self, 124–131
  psychology of, 70–75
  "time lock", 59–60
Climax, 33–34
Conflict, 49–51, 81–82
Creativity, 2–7, 10

D

Denouement, 86
Dialogue, 106–110
  emotional, 111–112

E

Emotional arc, 58–61
Emotions, 62–65, 111–112, 114–115,
    120–122
Episodic writing, 36
Exercises, 10, 19, 30, 38, 48, 57, 66, 76,
    87, 95, 105, 113, 123, 135,
    149, 152, 166
Exposition, 110–111, *see also* Script format

F

Free writing, 6–9

H

Hooking the audience, 27–28

I

Ideas, 2
Imagination, *see* Creativity

J

Jung, C. G., 131

M

Main character, *see* Protagonist
Maslow, A., 3
Motivation, 11–13, 15–17, 43–47, 59

O

Outline, *see* Step outline

P

Primary creativity, 2–3
Protagonist, 39–41, 55–56, *see also*
    Antagonist
  goal of, 61–62
  motivation, 43–47, 59

R

Rilke, R. M., 12

S

Scenes, 78–83, 91–92
Script format, 96–99, 100–104
  business, 99–100
Secondary creativity, 2–3
Step outline, 92–93
Story structure, 1, 20–21, 25–26, 31–33,
    35–36, 78, 83, 150
  climax, 33–34
  framework, 23–24, 26–27
  theme, 34–35
  topics, 22–23

Subtext, 114–118, 120–122
  in actions, 118–120
Survival, 153–165
  self–esteem, 157–158

T

Theme, 34–35
Time lock, 59–60
Treatment, 93–94

V

Visualization, 6–7, 23, 35, 68

W

Writer's block, 136–144
Writing, 4–9, 12–18, 22–28, 36–37, 77, 82,
    88, 106–107, 115, 124–125
  "don'ts", 15–17
  free writing, 6–9
  from the heart, 3–4, 8–9, 13, 62, 121,
    128
  journals, 4–6
  motives, 11–13, 15–17
  outline, 92–93
  personal, 13–15, 17–18
  professional, 15–17
  stumbling blocks, 144–148
  synopsis, 88–91
  treatment, 93–94
Writing exercises, 10, 19, 30, 38, 48, 57,
    66, 76, 87, 95, 105, 113, 123,
    135, 149, 152, 166